Black
Literature
and
Humanism
in
Latin
America

Richard L. Jackson

Black Literature and Humanism in Latin America

The University of Georgia Press

Athens and London

© 1988 by the University of Georgia Press
Athens, Georgia 30602
All rights reserved

Designed by Sandra Hudson
Set in Linotron 202 Meridien

The paper in this book meets the guidelines
for permanence and durability of the
Committee on Production Guidelines
for Book Longevity of the Council on
Library Resources.

Printed in the United States of America

92 91 90 89 88   5 4 3 2 1

Library of Congress Cataloging in
Publication Data

Jackson, Richard L., 1937–
    Black literature and humanism in Latin
    America.

Bibliography: p.
Includes index.
1. Latin American literature—Black
authors—History and criticism. 2. Latin
American literature—20th century—
History and criticism. 3. Blacks in literature.
4. Humanism in literature. I. Title.
PQ7081.J263   1988   860′.9′896
87-13290
ISBN 0-8203-0979-6 (alk. paper)

British Library Cataloging in Publication
Data available

To Chris (1964–1986), our firstborn, a fine son, an incredible big brother, and a very special person who showed such courage, tolerance, and inner strength during his painful four-month struggle to live, and who will be remembered with love, pride, admiration, and respect by all of us who were touched by his life and example.

Each black poet has
attempted . . . to express a black
humanism that would speak to the
inhumanity of his time.
—Richard Barksdale

Contents

Preface

The concept of humanism came under scrutiny recently in a series of conferences: "Black American Literature and Humanism," "Hispanism as Humanism," and "Africa and the West: The Challenge of African Humanism," held at the University of Tennessee campus in November 1978, at the University of New York at Albany in March 1980, and at the Ohio State University in May 1982 respectively. All of these conferences point in the direction I take this book, which generally is an exploration of the relationship of modern black literature to humanism and the quest for ethnic authenticity in Latin America. My specific purposes, however, are threefold: namely, to discuss the primary nature of this literature, which is its focus on the human condition; to underscore the relationship of black humanism to the evolving concept of literary Americanism in Latin America; and to highlight the humanistic impact of the black legacy in the literature of the area.

I accomplish these purposes by tracing the humanist vision in twentieth-century black Hispanic literature from the *Afrocriollo* movement in the 1920s, 1930s, and 1940s to the most recent literature written in Spanish and in some cases in Portuguese by blacks in Latin America today. In addition, I relate that vision not only to Latin American literature as a whole but to a general "return to the human" evident in recent literary criticism. This study not only complements and updates my previous work in Afro-Hispanic literature; it contributes as well to our understanding of this literature's role and place in Black Studies, Latin American Studies, and humanistic studies. With these disciplines in mind, I translate all quotes into English. Significant and substantial passages from several new black novels appear here in English for the first time.

For their feedback, I am especially grateful to students, colleagues, and audiences at Carleton University, the University of Tennessee,

Knoxville College, the University of Kentucky, Western Carolina University, York University, the College of Wooster, and to participants in symposia held in New York, El Paso, Claremont, and Washington, D.C., where I had opportunities to discuss much of this material. I also would like very much to thank the editors of the following publications (in which the articles below first appeared) for permission to incorporate these earlier versions in parts of this book: "Black Latin American Literature and Humanism," *Caribe* (1980); "*Chimurenga:* Literature and Black Liberation in Spanish America," *Repression and Liberation in Latin America* (1981); "Literary Blackness and Literary Americanism: Toward an Afro Model for Latin American Literature," *Afro-Hispanic Review* (1982); "The *Afrocriollo* Movement Revisited," *Afro-Hispanic Review* (1984); "The Human Legacy of Black Latin American Literature," *College Language Association Journal* (1986); "Coming Full Circle: The Polemical Trajectory of Modern Literary *americanismo*," *Inter-American Review of Bibliography* (1987); "Myth, History, and Narrative Structure in Manuel Zapata Olivella's *Changó, el gran putas*," *Revista/Review Interamericana* 13, nos. 1–4 (1983), a publication of Inter American University of Puerto Rico, San Germán; and "The Black Novel in Latin America Today," *Chasqui* (1987).

Introduction

The "Civilization of the twenty-first century" . . . will surely be humanism *or* barbarism *depending on whether or not the peoples of the Third World, and among them the black peoples, will have brought to it their contributions.*

—Léopold Sédar Senghor

In a recent lecture at the University of Tennessee, Professor Charles H. Long reportedly spoke on the need to reconstruct the meanings of primitivism and civilization, a process, he advised, that would enhance the definition of humanism. I was immediately struck by the juxtaposition of the words *primitivism, civilization,* and *humanism* when I learned of his comments, because at the time I had this work underway on black literature and Latin America's own dichotomy regarding primitivism and civilization, or between civilization and "barbarism," as it is called in that part of the world. Humanism throughout this study is understood simply to mean an attitude of concern for the welfare and dignity of human beings, especially the "marginal" ones, and for the problems that beset them in this life.

The meanings of civilization and barbarism in Latin America are under reconstruction. Nineteenth-century Hispanic slavery was hardly a humanizing experience,[1] which is why this reconstruction has been long in coming. Nevertheless, ethnic and cultural symbols are slowly being reversed not only in literature by blacks but in other recent literature from the area as well. Consistent with this reversal I use the term *ethnocentrism,* but not in the normal Eurocentric sense applying to those who "by racial privilege or education or both"[2] exclude nonwhites from the "mainstream." Rather I turn the term around and apply it Afrocentrically[3] to the body of literature about and especially by these formerly excluded peoples. With this reversal in mind I explore the humanist legacy of black literature in Latin America.

Black literature in Latin America can be defined within the theoretical framework of *ethnopoetics*, a term associated with oral traditions and with new forms of poetry created when oral and preliterate forms merge with written or formal languages. The term itself is relatively new, but ethnopoetic expression has been around for a long time in Latin America. Early Spanish church fathers tried to stamp out native Indian literature, but some of it persisted. *Gaucho* literature flourished in the nineteenth century, and black literature had a slow start but gained impetus in the early twentieth century when the search for the primitive gave "black" poetry high visibility. At that time many observers cast doubts on Western civilization, which they saw in decline, and they sought something of value, even possibilities for a "new beginning," in the "primitive" but enviable black. Ethnopoetics expresses similar doubts about Western (white) civilization.

Inherent in ethnopoetics is a redefinition of the word *primitive*, which makes this term, like *ethnocentrism* the way I understand it, extremely relevant to the reversal of symbols taking place in Latin America where since early in this century there has been a tendency toward the incorporation of marginal (nonwhite) cultures into literature. Ethnopoetics defines literature normally exiled from the mainstream of white civilization in America. In search of a truly "American voice," Latin American authors have gone back to a "poetry of sources, of a fundamental human nature,"[4] an inevitable move that humanizes literature by including the "marginal" contributions of the formerly excluded.[5]

Many Latin American authors early in this century seemed to believe that "all the old excluded orders must be included . . . all that has been outcast and vagabond must return to be admitted in the creation of what we consider we are."[6] *Afrocriollista, indigenista,* and other *mundonovista* authors rejected the belief that "the allegorical figure of the people of Latin America, was 'blond and white,' "[7] and they returned to the roots in search of "who we are, and where . . . we have come from."[8] In this search for a new "poetic and human base"[9] the distance between "marginal" black literature and the larger Latin American literature of which it forms a part was considerably reduced.

The *ethnos*, or the human part, of the term *ethnopoetics* normally suggests cultures that are remote, exotic, and different, even "tribal if we are not tribal, religious if we are secular, dark if we are light, etc."[10] *Ethnos* implies a poetics of the Other, but what I suggest in this book is that the traditional Other, while different, is essentially and simultaneously the same, and representative. Ethnopoetics is a human poetics, thus its relevance to the humanist legacy of Afro–Latin American literature. Futhermore, ethnopoetics has to be seen, as Sylvia Wynter sees it,[11] in the context of *sociopoetics* as well, where the revolutionary and proletarian consciousness of the *socio* is given as much weight as the folk emphasis of the *ethno*. The humanist legacy relates to both, and through black literature in Latin America we can address the relationship between the First World (Europe) and the Third World. Ethnopoetics is a poetics "of the Other," but it is also a poetics "of our kind" and "of who we are".

Black literature in Latin America is definitely Afro-centered but it is also Latin American. Since most Latin American countries, it has been argued, are not "wholly white,"[12] black literature can be representative especially when it reflects such universal themes as liberation, identity, and struggle shared by a large part of humanity. The black experience is one of the most universal experiences the world has ever known "because it includes all the pain, sorrow, hardships and frustrations that are fundamental to man."[13] For this reason we not only identify the humanist legacy of black Latin American literature; we explore as well what that legacy has to offer on a larger Latin American and universal level.

This study, in short, approaches literary Americanism in Latin America largely through black Hispanic models that in many ways make up a microcosm of the larger literature. Viewing Latin American literature from within a distinct ethnic group considered marginal is consistent with the search for authenticity in Latin America where Latin American specificity, or *la especificidad latinoamericana*, often is identified, at least symbolically, with African and indigenous cultures. Literature about blacks by blacks themselves, whether written in the Spanish-speaking part of Latin America or in Brazil, is clearly distinguishable in theme, focus, and purpose from Latin American literature about blacks by nonblack authors.

Recognition of the existence in Brazil of a specifically black, or Afro-Brazilian, vision of the role of blacks and black culture is one of the major achievements of David Brookshaw's valuable new book *Race and Color in Brazilian Literature*.[14] Brookshaw finds this to be true despite the occasional adulation of white as an aesthetic ideal by some black Brazilian writers. Even while recognizing, for example, Jorge Amado's long commitment to Afro-Brazilian culture Brookshaw questions the authenticity of his portrayals of Afro-Brazilians. Amado, Brazil's most prestigious and widely known exponent of Afro-Brazilian culture, has defended blacks but does not, he contends, achieve the depth of characterization evoked by writers who are themselves Afro-Brazilian.

Brookshaw laments the conspicious absence of black writers in Brazil, "with arguably the largest black population of any country outside of Africa" (p. 175), of the fame and caliber of Langston Hughes, James Baldwin, Richard Wright, and Ralph Ellison. Yet, while discussing the absence of a distinct black literary tradition in Brazil, he does give an in-depth analysis of the work of earlier Afro-Brazilian authors and such contemporary black Brazilian writers as Solano Trindade, Eduardo de Oliveira, Abdias do Nascimento, and Deoscóredes M. dos Santos (Didi), among others. Another given derived from his analyses of these writers is that much of this Afro-Brazilian literature contains the seed of a new humanism in Latin America. This assessment underscores my own contention that authentic black literature in Latin America, stressing as it does the worth, value, and welfare of human beings, can be taken as an ideal model or prototype for any literature aspiring to these humanistic concerns. The larger Latin American literature is no exception.

My first chapter, "The Authenticity Question," reviews the modern trajectory of literary Americanism in Latin America. Chapter 2, "From Black Folk Up," explores the black roots of modern literary Americanism. Chapter 3, "Modern Black Heroism," continues this discussion by focusing on the heroic tradition in black literature in Latin America. Chapter 4, "The Great New *Mandinga*," discusses the humanist values of black literary models in Latin America which, as defenders of liberty and guardians of national cultures, set thematic and historical standards to be emulated. Chapter 5, "The Continuing Quest," and chapter 6, "The

Shango Saga," update the humanist vision of black Latin American literature as we can trace it in some of the most recent novels written by blacks in Latin America today.

In chapter 5 I focus on Carlos Guillermo Wilson ("Cubena") and Quince Duncan in Central America, Nelson Estupiñán Bass in Ecuador, and Jorge Artel and Juan Zapata Olivella in Colombia, and in chapter 6 on their Afro-Colombian counterpart Manuel Zapata Olivella. These six writers exemplify important tendencies developing in recent Afro-Hispanic fiction, namely, black pride and an increasing identification with Africa as well as with literary Americanism, class solidarity, and Third Worldism. What they have in common with each other, with Nicolás Guillén, and with other Afro–Latin American authors, however, is far more significant: a legacy characterized by a quest for human rights and freedoms. The whole of chapter 6 is given over to Zapata Olivella's account of this quest and the African spirit that motivated it.

Chapter 7 "Toward a Human Poetics," provides an overview of some advocates of criticism based on principles of humanistic analysis. Also in this final chapter I emphasize that Black Studies must have an international perspective which, like criticism itself, should be humanistic. I define Black Studies as humanism in action, and since humanistic advocacy is a coveted stance in Latin American literature it seemed appropriate to close by relating Black Studies, the black legacy, and black literature in Latin America to the kind of human poetics surfacing in the recent literary criticism, for example, of Eugene Goodheart, John Gardner, and John Reichert.

Chapter One

The Authenticity Question

The quest for authenticity is one of the most important aspects of Spanish-American literature.

—Jean Franco

The Human Climate

At the beginning of this century Latin American literature underwent an important transformation. White writers at that time turned the concept of literary Americanism away from exclusive preoccupation with their own identity vis-à-vis Europe and toward other human types found in America. While black authors wrote about their own experiences, other writers reflected the social tragedy of the continent by calling for the necessary integration of all into national life. Concerned authors, particularly novelists, tried to show what it was like to be human in that part of the world, and they exposed human suffering and other dehumanizing qualities of life that threaten man's dignity. Even racist authors whose works betrayed their heritage of white racial consciousness could not avoid bringing indigenous and African elements into literature.

Miguel Angel Asturias once said that Latin American literature is a literature invaded by life. This "public service" interest in social and racial problems in Latin American societies, ironically, left many of the early novelists in this century in disrepute stylistically. But though some of the acknowledged old classics have been outdistanced technically by the much-heralded new novel, ethnic types (or the *elemento nuevo* these earlier novelists introduced into Latin American literature), even when distorted and abused, lay at the core of what was to become an ongoing

1

search for a literary common denominator, a search that has provided an organizing principle for many authors since.

Whether called *constantes, claves, rasgos predominantes,* a *signo latinoamericano, la especificidad latinoamericana,* or indeed a *denominador común,* the intent has been the same, namely, to find the *hecho central* that explains and gives cohesion to Latin American literature. Fernando Ainsa[1] and Augusto Roa Bastos[2] used the same term, *centro de cohesión interior,* for their search, especially the latter, who, quoting António Cândido's reference to a necessary *estructura interior armónica,* spoke of the need for a distinctive central core in literature that goes beyond aesthetic value. These constants, Roa Bastos argued, derive from *contextos,* or external factors, that enrich literary expression. Just what these enrichment factors, embodied in the *signo latinoamericano,* are has given rise to a long polemical discussion of Latin American literature. In addition to ethnic types, such constants as social protest, *mestizaje,* nature, language, violence, magic realism, conflict, and civilization and barbarism have all been put forward from time to time as more constant than others. Whatever the choice, human relevance has often been the key, and the plight of the common person a very popular subject.

Many topics addressed during the *historia polémica* concerned the novel, and among the early critics two of the most prominent were Arturo Torres Rioseco and Luis Alberto Sánchez. The polemical history did not intensify, however, until the late 1940s when Pedro Grases[3] and José Antonio Portuondo,[4] among others, identified what they saw as constants in Latin American literature, namely, nature and social protest, respectively. The polemical history will continue, but already in the 1940s the search for a common denominator had raised important aesthetic issues. Portuondo considered *lo social* to be one aspect of the concept of literary Americanism. But in doing so he also raised another issue that was to become equally contentious, namely, the concept of literature itself. While viewing literature as a social document, Portuondo was careful to insist that works of art, even when they are "documents," never reflect reality as it is but as seen through the creative spirit of the author. What literature reflects, Portuondo argued, is not reality per se but the author's vision of it. When that vision is humanistic, as was often the intent for many of the social protest or public service novelists, the personal focus on social reality heightened. Even the most artistically inclined writer, Portuondo insisted, was not completely out of touch with reality in Latin America.

Portuondo's predominant points—that literature in Latin America does not exist in an abstract vacuum and that social preoccupation with human reality is central to the concept of literary Americanism—underscore a dominant Latin American response to human questions. This response in prose is especially evident among the *mundonovista* novelists writing during the first half of this century. Acceptance of the humanistic challenge in an area noted for division, conflict, injustice, and other contentious aspects of the human drama emphasized that the advocacy function of literature was their first requirement.

Perhaps no one has explained the aesthetics of the *mundonovista* novelists better than Miguel Angel Asturias, who in conversation with Luis Harss outlined what he saw as a fundamental difference between the Latin American novelist and his European counterpart. The European novelist, he says, "has to a certain extent overcome the pull of nature. Therefore he can devote himself to exploring the complex problems of individual psychology. On the other hand, the domain of the Latin American novelists is still to a considerable extent the green hell populated by the human plants of the naturalist school. Our fiction is therefore largely a social and economic geography of the continent. Its mission is to digest, evaluate and criticize."[5]

Here Asturias links such common denominators as nature and protest by emphasizing the human climate of Latin America and the combative nature of its literature. Asturias reemphasizes his main point by asserting that the function of the early twentieth-century novel was "to expose the suffering of our people." And he adds: "I think it's difficult for this type of literature to be purely literary, to be concerned merely with what is beautiful or pleasing to the eyes or ears."[6] There is a human commitment in the works of Asturias, whose contributions to literary Americanism are obvious. The betterment of America was a basic theme in Asturias, which is why he rejected formalistic literature when it was concerned less with making people better than with what was beautiful and pleasing to the eyes and ears. Perhaps the outstanding value of the *mundonovista* novelists in the early part of this century was their acceptance of the belief that literature was related to life or it was nothing, that extraliterary *contextos* were just as important to the reader as the aesthetic experience, and that there can be no lasting human interest or meaningful aesthetic value in literature without human content. In short, to the *mundonovista* novelist, whether *indigenista, socio-negrista,* black, or novelist of the Mexican Revolution, humanism and literary Americanism ostensibly were one and the same thing.

"In the Plural Humanly"

Though much of the *historia polémica* focused on the novel (both of the *mundonovista* novelists—the first "new" novelists in this century—and of the more recent "new" novelists), some of the same issues were raised regarding poetry as well.[7] Modernism, for example, gave rise to many relevant polemics, among them its relationship to humanism and literary Americanism. The essence of modernism, some have argued, lay in a genuine Americanism that was reflected—ironically, as Federico de Onís explained—even in the foreign yearning of some of the modernist poets.[8] By turning, for example, to French models, Spanish America not only declared its independence from the excesses of romanticism and from Spanish forms, but also established through this kind of literary emancipation the cosmopolitan outlook associated with Latin American literature today. Foreign yearning in this sense became as typically American as *gaucho* literature, for example, or New Worldism in general.

Modernism, it is often said, moved from a first stage of antihumanism to a second stage where humanism and literary Americanism or New Worldism and its New World concerns become more important than aestheticism. The *mundonovista* poets, the later Rubén Darío among them, reflected humanistic concerns that took precedence over remote exotic allusions prevalent in the first stage of modernism. Several modernist poets fit this mold. Manuel González Prada, José Martí, José Santos Chocano, Rubén Darío, and Leopoldo Lugones, for example, became standard-bearers who attempted to identify with the social reality of the common people. The result, for the most part, was artificial or unauthentic identification from the outside.

José Santos Chocano was known as the "Poet of America," and his *Alma América* (1906) was instrumental in fomenting *mundonovismo*, or New Worldism. But Darío, following (like Santos Chocano) in the tradition of Andrés Bello and José Martí, already had begun in his *Cantos de vida y esperanza* (1905) to publicly recognize the need to come down from the ivory tower. In a real sense Darío not only fomented the spirit of renovation and innovation continued with Vicente Huidobro, César Vallejo, and Pablo Neruda and other later twentieth-century poets; he also stands in the tradition of humanism and literary Americanism continued by some of these same poets. What is more, Rubén Darío also pointed toward the "Vernacular American" or "the American Voice" that comes to fruition in a later response to dependency.

Tilting toward the "Vernacular American," Rubén Darío wrote: "If there is poetry in our America, you will find it in the old things, in Palenque and Utatlán, in the Indian."[9] Darío, of mixed African-Indian-Spanish ancestry, realized he had to go to the *muchedumbre* (multitude): "In spite of my cosmopolitan outlook, there is an enduring ethnic vein deep down in my being; my way of thinking and feeling continues a traditional and historic process."[10] It has been argued that Darío is a poet of race. This title, which can apply to his identification with Spain in his defense of *"España fecunda,"* and to the poet as a racially mixed Nicaraguan in close affinity to new-world peoples and concerns, suggests that Darío's literary Americanism resides not just in his cultural and literary synthesis but in his racial synthesis as well, a possibility that has been raised despite an ambivalence in Darío that brands some of his literary output—particularly in his prose—as racist.[11]

The "absence of human content,"[12] which characterized the spirit of aestheticism that prevailed in the "first" stage of modernism, killed the movement, certainly that phase of it. José Enrique Rodó, the author of this theory, equated modernism and antihumanism and by extension humanism and literary Americanism. Rodó was, of course, too hasty in his exclusion of Darío from the later development of modernism toward humanism and literary Americanism. He was on the right track, however, in his implication that any literary movement that stands outside the "human obligation of struggle"[13] is doomed to extinction.

Spanish-American poets have paid increasing attention to indigenous subjects and, like Darío, have been demonstrating that in them "there is poetry."[14] Indeed, the twentieth-century beginnings of literary Americanism can be traced back in part not only to the *Afrocriollista* movement in the 1920s and 1930s, as we shall see, but also to the "second," or "*mundonovista*," stage of modernism as well, which is why the *amor humanista* of César Vallejo, Pablo Neruda, and Nicolás Guillén is not too unlike the "essential humanism" associated with the later Darío.

For these true giants of Latin American poetry, as for the *mundonovista* novelists, humanism and literary Americanism were one and the same thing. America stood at the center of their concerns as their poetry evolved toward the strong interest in human solidarity we see expressed in much of their later work. Their skill in combining such concerns with artistic expression is largely responsible for the universal human interest that their poetry commands. All four of these poets (Vallejo, Neruda, Guillén, Rubén Darío) moved from self-contemplation and love of women and family to the larger concern for collective and oppressed humanity. On this broader humanistic impulse they built their concept of literary Americanism, which was opposed to human misery and adapted to the needs of the specific human realities they took as their points of departure, namely, the black, the Indian, and all the victimized of America to whom, about whom, and for whom Neruda sang his "Universal Song."

These poets responded to human problems both creatively and politically. The result has been personal involvement not only in political life and ideology but also in what I would call a human poetics, best summed up as a communal stance reflected, for example, in Vallejo's poem "Masa," which could be regarded as the ultimate humanistic statement in Latin American literature. The communal stance in this poem can be set against any of the poems these writers wrote before their humanistic conversions when they were writing poetry that reflected not an interest in human solidarity or collective struggle against human misery but the "solitary self" or the "self in solitude."

From the solitary self, then, to feeling "in the plural, humanly,"[15] these poets drew on their roots in America to build an essential humanism that gives body to abstract philosophical concepts and political ideologies. Though believing that bolshevism, or communism, is humanism in action, Vallejo also believed strongly in the originality of national or Indian cultures "and the need for any form of government to be rooted in them."[16] As with Darío, some of Vallejo's admirers are firmly convinced that Vallejo, too, can be considered a poet of race,[17] and that an Indian influence makes his poetry authentically American and original. They link his hatred of suffering to the mistreatment of the Indian who, in Vallejo's work, becomes a symbol of man and a prototype of the human condition. Vallejo obviously writes a universal poetry, but to some the humanistic compassion that characterizes it is linked to an autochthonous element represented by the Peruvian Indian.

Neruda's love of humanity was later built on his opposition to the human misery suffered by the American. His well-known conversion was inspired by human suffering in Spain, but throughout his career Neruda's humanistic vision focused on "our American world,"[18] on "our American home."[19] Neruda attempted to write in his *Canto general* (1950) the ultimate epic statement on human liberty and the American people. The humanistic impulse is certainly the cornerstone of "Macchu Picchu," the core of this epic, where he exhorts his *hermano*, "Sube a nacer conmigo,"[20] and where he continually inquires about the human race. Throughout his poetry Neruda insists that his song is "for the people" and that as a poet of the people he sees himself as "mankind's accomplice."[21] Whether Neruda is talking in the abstract or concretely, *lo humano* becomes the common denominator of his poetry.

Human communication explains the conversational nature of much of the poetry of Vallejo and Neruda and also justifies, as we shall see, Nicolás Guillén's incorporation of oral or folk forms from the Afro-Cuban experience into his formal literature. This desire to communicate clearly led the Cuban poet to speak as a "true Black"[22] and Neruda to

insist: "Let us speak simply."[23] Neruda's continuing interest in humanistic expression was presaged years ago when he wrote that "any creation that is not in the service of liberty in these days of total menace
[Nazism], is treason,"[24] and when he dismissed Borges as too preoccupied with problems "that are not interesting to me because they are
not human."[25]

While it may be true that "in Chile and, indeed, in all of Latin America,
contemporary poetry begins with Vicente Huidobro,"[26] the creationism
of his fellow countryman was not shared by Neruda, who opposed
Huidobro's dictum that a poet is a "little god." Huidobro's emphasis on
the creation of alternate worlds and on the power of language to fashion
an absolute self-referential poetic reality represented the antithesis of
Neruda's humanistic view of the social reality of America. Huidobro is
extremely significant, however, for the concept of literature as creation
and diversion that was to become popular with the new novelists: his
aesthetics of creationism represented the central issue or the line of de-
marcation drawn in the battle of the ancient and the modern. In this
battle an art for people's sake—literary Americanism—was challenged
by an art for art's sake that moved Latin America onto center stage and
into the universal mainstream.

The "Terrible Dilemma"

In moving into the mainstream, Latin America experienced a boom in
literature and in criticism. Poets, intellectuals, and critics like Pablo
Neruda, Jorge Luis Borges, and Octavio Paz were among the signal figures, but the new novel and its reception caused the critical stir that
precipitated the Latin American version of the battle between the ancient and the modern. This battle, simply put, stemmed from the characterization of the new novel as a technically advanced and universal form
of writing as opposed to the *mundonovista* novel, dismissed by the sons
as primitive, provincial, and technically uninspiring. But the fathers also
disowned the sons, seeing in the new novel a continuation of ivory

tower dehumanization dating back to the first stage of modernism and particularly to the vanguardism of Huidobro, who, seemingly ahead of his time, spoke of the superior value of a world created by language over one based upon mimetic reflection of existing reality.

At stake here, of course, was the concept of humanism, as the new novel, with its emphasis on form, language, and structure, came to represent for some a private and individual kind of literature as play. The close association of such playful spirits as Borges and the Mexican Salvador Elizondo with the new novel did not discourage this image. Borges is well known for his "game" literature, and Elizondo's esoteric terminology and difficult texts, coupled with his lack of interest in Mexico, certainly set him apart from the *mundonovista* novelists and from such humanistic poets as Neruda and Nicolás Guillén. It is hardly likely, for example, that either of these two poets would ever make such a statement as the one made recently by Elizondo: "I'd never want to write about Mexico."[27] With the advent of Borges, the new novelists, and extremists like Elizondo, the advocacy tradition associated with the earlier "committed" novelists became threatened. We will examine the new response to this threat, but the foundation of that discussion, indeed the rationale for the new response itself, is related to the characterization of the old and the new novel that set off the battle in the first place.

The twentieth-century Latin American novel has been grouped under such headings as modern and contemporary, realism and super-realism, "before Asturias and after Asturias," novels of the city and novels of the land, and perhaps most popularly, the primitive novel and the creative novel, the one old and traditional and the other new and innovative. In addition to being old, traditional, and primitive, the earlier *mundonovista* novel has been charged at one time or another with being conventional, simplistic, Manichean, content-oriented, ideological, impure, regional, realistic, ontological, social, *verosímil*, native, explicit, didactic, documentary, spatial, mimetic, referential, moral, formulistic, closed, persuasive, subjective, and humanistic—and with using language as a means to an end. The new novel, on the other hand, in addition to being new, creative, and innovative, has been characterized as being experimental, scientific, textual, ambiguous, complex, artistic, form- and craft-oriented, pure, universal, autotelic, organic, autonomous, formalistic, dehumanized, cosmopolitan, avant-garde, diverse, implicit, self-referential, imaginative, super-realistic, linguistic, mythic, open, and objective—and with being a *roman puzzle* that uses language as an end in itself, namely, the creation of an alternative verbal reality.

The bottom line in the aspect of the *historia polémica* represented by the battle between generations is that humanistic advocacy with the new novelists became less obvious than with their forebears. The earlier novelists' concept of liberty was a social, collective, and humanistic one, unlike the new novelists' aesthetic, which emphasized the artistic and individual freedom of the artist, who saw himself at liberty to create as he desired. The linguistic liberties the new novelists took with language, structure, and form gave the impression to many of their detractors that humanistic advocacy was less important to them than linguistic play. Rather than blatantly reflecting life or reality as the "traditionals" did, the new novelists were accused of avoiding it, an accusation even spokesmen and supporters of the boom did not discourage.

The linguistic and artistic innovations of the new novelists, when patterned on foreign literary models, were equated by some with betrayal, political sellout, avoidance of external Latin American reality in favor of more internal and thus universal visions and cosmopolitan settings, and with dependency. This development away from the Latin American *esencia* and the human realities on which it is based and toward an objective reality intensified the *choque de generaciones,* or the generation gap. Mario Benedetti widened that gap when he wrote:

It is curious how the Latin American critic living in Europe generally opts for formalist or structuralist criticism when writing about Latin America. This option, of course, could be legitimate, but the abundance of examples we can point to leads to the suspicion that in some cases this almost fanatical interest in forms, structures and signifiers might be a way of avoiding content, meaning and the demands of the real world.[28]

Benedetti also charged that there were some Latin American writers—not just those who live in Europe—who wrote with the "transparent intention"[29] of being read by structuralist critics. Benedetti can be counted among more recent Latin American critics who call for a literature more attuned to the ethnic reality of Latin America, particularly to its *mestizo* background.

Earlier classifications of the novel by Arturo Torres Rioseco[30] and Luis Alberto Sánchez[31] highlighted such ethnic figures as the Indian, the *gaucho*, and the black. Later classifications, however, by Fernando Alegría,[32] Zunilda Gertel,[33] Cedomil Goic,[34] and Mario Vargas Llosa,[35] to mention only a few, use aesthetic categories based on movements, forms, periods, and style. This move away from social reality toward the other, invented, reality inspired Ramón Xirau's "Crisis of Realism,"[36] Jorge Enrique Adoum's "The Realism of the Other Reality,"[37] and other studies that dealt with what really became a major concern among novelists and critics, namely, how should Latin American authors write?

The quick answer to this question has already been intimated in our summary of the "old" and the "new" novelists. If we isolate from that summary comparison the two words *formulistic* (taken to mean didactic protest clichés of social realism) and *formalistic* (meaning innovative, stylistic, and artistic), we have in the first instance what Latin American authors should avoid and in the second that to which they should aspire.[38] The linguistic innovations of the new novel, however, gave some critics the impression that it was becoming a literature of evasion. The problem with the new novel as Benedetti saw it was that it was interested more in revolution in language than in any other kind of revolution, and in literary *engagement* more than in social *engagement*.[39] In short, commitment, it seemed to him, was more to literature than to the kinds of causes humanistic writers long felt it their moral duty to champion.

Language, Fernández Retamar argued, became for many new novelists an end in itself, and their new novels a "do-it-yourself experience"[40] where the medium became the message. Baroque expression, the dissolution of genres as we know them, and intertextuality, or the use of others' texts in one's own, in a sense became the ultimate evasion where reference was to the textual creations of other writers rather than to direct reality. The barriers such "hermetic and frivolous art for the select few"[41] erected prevented easy communication; they also presented a dilemma for new novelists accused of writing only "market-able" literature for foreign consumption. The argument against the verbal or structuralist realism of the new novel in Latin America, in short, was that "independent" literary Americanism had been replaced with a "dependent" literary Europeanism.

Although the revolution in language the new novel represented corresponded roughly, as some like to point out, with the revolution in Cuba—the two ostensibly ushering in a whole new political, cultural, and literary look in Latin America—such authors as Fernández Retamar and Mario Benedetti were critical of the new novel. Other critics even harsher in their judgments—Manuel Pedro González, Oscar Collazos, Hernán Vidal, to name only a few—saw the new novel as language gone astray or as an abuse of sophistication.

Manuel Pedro González praised the authenticity of the *mundonovista* novelists and became the most virulent critic of what he called "the intellectual servilism" of the new novel.[42] In a devil's advocate role, the Mexican author drew very clearly the battle lines between the *choque de generaciones*. With his charges of "empty formalism," and "intellectual parricide" Manuel Pedro González moved the polemical history into high gear in 1966 at an important symposium at the University of Washington where he declared that the true Latin American writer must not only live in his or her country but must write about it as well and in a style not dependent on a foreign aesthetic.[43] González insisted that he was not against artistic value in prose or against technical innovation provided it is homegrown, authentic, and faithful to the concept of literary Americanism. González saw such qualities in the earlier novelists, who had their faults, he admitted, but who were in touch with and reflected the telluric and ethnic realities of "our America" and did so, he added, "using forms that were fitting and much more artistic and innovative than anything that had been done before."[44]

The literary arguments in the 1940s focused interest on the concept of literary Americanism, and the symposium in 1966 moved the debate along. There were other celebrated clashes, however, particularly the contrasting views, published in 1970, held by Oscar Collazos, Julio Cortázar, and Mario Vargas Llosa[45] where Collazos takes up the devil's advocate role played earlier by Manuel Pedro González. Whereas González's targets included the critics Ivan Schulman and Fernando Alegría, Collazos took on the new novelists themselves represented by Cortázar and Vargas Llosa. Collazos's argument was much the same as his predecessor's, namely, that some new novelists were out of touch and more concerned with foreign consumption than with Latin American reality. Collazos belittled the new novelists and their verbal skill, arguing that writers should identify with the Cuban Revolution. Some Latin American intellectuals highly politicized in their view of literature saw the boom as a manifestation of the dependency theory; that is, "as a phenomenon more or less manufactured and advertised in the United States through collaboration between certain of the boom authors themselves and U.S. publishers and critics for the mutual benefit of all concerned."[46]

Hernán Vidal saw the boom in this fashion. The Chilean critic used marketing terms to define the new novel as a literary form that "reflects and responds to the new phase of Latin American dependency, namely, the economic influence of the multinational conglomerates, especially those based in the United States."[47] Vidal was especially critical of the formalistic nature of the new novel. Opposing intellectual parricide, he took Carlos Fuentes and Mario Vargas Llosa to task for rejecting the earlier literature as primitive and for giving the impression that the new novel had no antecedents, that it was born in a vacuum with no literary tradition behind it. The new novel, to Vidal, was a middle-class product written for middle-class consumption, with no insight into class struggle or responsible political action beneficial to Latin American literature and history. The foreign pressures exerted on this novel, he argued, left it without the capacity to "humanize its space."[48]

There is some irony involved at this level of the debate. The new novel, some believed, owed its beginning to momentum generated by the Cuban Revolution, but came, at its zenith, to be identified with all the revolution despised, namely, capitalist values and "colonial" models. The freedom of Cuba, the argument went, led to the freedom to experiment in literature. But this artistic license, in turn, gave rise to "the crisis of the liberal imagination,"[49] in which "even when an author appeared to be holding society up to criticism, the very structures of the narrative reproduced its assumption."[50] Simplistically put, the new novel, for those who chart literary movements against historical events, came to an end with the downfall of Allende in 1973, which symbolized, they argue, the final betrayal or sellout to a "dangerous kind of modernity,"[51] one that removes Latin America too far from its revolutionary and social advocacy base which earlier identification with the Cuban Revolution had perpetuated.

Manuel Pedro González, Oscar Collazos, and Hernán Vidal took issue not only with the new novel as an art form but with the new novelists themselves. Cortázar, Vargas Llosa, and Carlos Fuentes are authors of well-known critical statements regarding the new novel. Cortázar's call for more revolutionaries of language than for intellectuals in the revolution comes to mind, as does Carlos Fuentes's characterization of the new novel as more complex, ambiguous, and universal than the old novel. We also have Vargas Llosa's often-cited classification of the old novelists and the new novelists as "primitives" and "creators."

The new novelist-as-critic most attacked was Carlos Fuentes. Roberto Fernández Retamar, Marta Sánchez,[52] and Carlos Blanco Aguinaga[53] all criticized the Mexican author's rejection of the traditional novels and his eagerness to impose universal myths and foreign models on the Latin American novel. This eagerness blinded Fuentes to the fact, Sánchez charged, that Azuela's Los de abajo was the first Mexican novel to have no European model. Sánchez lamented as well that Fuentes would link Rulfo's Pedro Páramo to Greek myth rather than to Mexico's own past heritage. In short, some saw the new novelists' technique in criticism as in fiction as an escape which impeded or discouraged "any direct confrontation with the historical content embodied in these novels."[54]

This striving for modernity, or, to paraphrase Octavio Paz, to be contemporary or up-to-date with the world, presented the new novelists with such dilemmas as which ideological side to take and, indeed, with the choice between political commitment and the creation of a truly autonomous fictional world. The dilemma that most confronted the new novelists involved breaking with the past and thus running the risk of "betraying" the humanistic tradition in Latin America in favor of opening up new avenues artistically. But even when that tradition was honored, as with José María Arguedas, the question of authenticity was still crucial to the concept of literary Americanism as its newest interpreters would define it.

Mario Vargas Llosa introduced us to the authenticity question in a recent statement on the Latin American writer in general and José María Arguedas's personal dilemma in particular.[55] Vargas Llosa is one of José María Arguedas's fondest admirers. His fellow Peruvian, who killed himself December 2, 1969, chose suicide, Vargas Llosa explains, as a way out of the "terrible dilemma" of the Latin American writer, namely, the choice between taking a position in the ivory tower or in the streets, between responding to humanistic questions morally and responsibly or isolating oneself from society, its people, and its problems to write beautiful literature about an autonomous, created fictional world. Arguedas tried to be humanistic and authentic by writing about the Indian from within, using the Indian's own manner of expression. That Arguedas believed he had failed on both counts and chose suicide as the honorable response to his "failure" is open to speculation.

What is not open to speculation is that Arguedas did experience that "terrible dilemma"; his suicide was "in a way, showing how difficult and daring it can be to be a writer in Latin America."[56] Vargas Llosa understood, as Arguedas did, that social conditions force a moral choice on the writer, and to betray this obligation is to risk being considered a deserter and a traitor. Vargas Llosa also implied that authors in Latin America must in the first instance produce a literature "in touch with living reality, with the experiences of the people."[57] While he recognized the dangers inherent in a morally simplistic approach to literature, Vargas Llosa remained antagonistic toward the proliferation of "textual" literature of formal experimentation in Latin America. Structuralist or formalist criticism, he has said, "is a type of criticism that interests me very little and bores me a great deal."[58] This post–new novel statement points very well toward recent critics who call for a new humanism and a new response to dependency in Latin America.

The New Response

This new response to dependency and the parallel call for a new humanism are not unrelated developments, and both, in turn, point to an ever-sought *especificidad latinoamericana*. They relate as well to increasing recognition of the need for a "new criticism adapted to Latin American reality,"[59] a humanistic criticism, the argument goes, that would put more stress on Latin American *contextos* and less on schemata, diagrams, and formulas that dehumanize and detract from the text. This new response cautions that a criticism for an underdeveloped area need not be an underdeveloped criticism, or a *"subcrítica literaria."*[60] One indispensable element a new criticism or theory of Latin American literature would require is that it be authentic, with criteria based on Latin American reality and not on a "psuedo-universality" associated with Europe and the United States.

The word *authenticity* is crucial to the supporters of this new response. Angel Rama has spoken of *diversión auténtica,* José Antonio Portuondo of *cultura auténtica,* and Noé Jitrik of *autenticidad social.* Authenticity in each case can be applied to authors who write about subjects close to the real concerns of their Latin American readers without falling prey to the cult of foreign models. Central to the new response is the desire to replace veneration for the foreign and disdain for one's own with the desire to develop not an autonomous literary world of fiction but an "autonomous culture."[61] To the advocates of the new response Cuba, in this sense, "offers a standard against which other Latin American societies may be compared in their progress toward cultural independence."[62]

Participants in the new response do not reject outright or downgrade the earlier *mundonovista* novelists as the new novelists and their critics did. On the contrary, they see the traditional or primitive novel as having fulfilled an important stage—*una etapa necesaria,*[63] in the words of António Cândido—in that it focused on the kinds of human problems of the dispossessed still operable in Latin America. Though conceding that dependency is unavoidable in the use of imported literary forms, Cândido expects themes, sentiments, and concerns to be regional and national, however stylized the language. He does not expect Latin American writers to reject the sonnet and free verse, for example, but he does expect them to inject Latin American life into these forms. In this new response the argument sustained is that those who accept outside influence should impose a Latin American frame of reference on their literature even when technical treatment is influenced from the outside.

Another argument opposes the adoption of foreign critical standards: "We must create our own critical focus,"[64] cry the architects of the new response, who reject authors not "committed to their homelands."[65] Latin American literature should not be judged on foreign terms, they argue, for to do so is to do an injustice to that literature. Robert Mead addressed this problem when he wrote of this "truly difficult and ultimately impossible task: to evaluate with intelligence, subtlety, and in depth a work born of another way of life, the work of a man of a different culture,"[66] unless that man is Jorge Luis Borges. For Mead, and for some of the Argentine author's detractors, Borges represents the sort of writer—cosmopolitan and universal in theme, clear in language and metaphysical in context—who appeals to English-language readers. Younger writers in Latin America searching for the roots of their national identity and concerned with the social and moral issues of their continent do not, Mead believes, read Borges the way their fathers did, although they do honor him as a pioneering master.[67]

Theories, systems, critical methodologies, and standards from other literatures and cultures, then, are taboo in the new response, a post–new novel period characterized more by emphasis on the human essence of Latin America than on language, technique, and foreign models. The content and ideology resident in the innovative prose, for example, of Cortázar, Fuentes, and Carpentier often revealed, Marta Sánchez charges, a continuing identification "with the cultural and literary models of the dominant bourgeoisies of the First World."[68] What this means, she contends, is that these authors define *lo americano* only within terms of reference of "mainstream criticism," that is, only with reference to "universal" dominant models. In short, Sánchez suggests, their position is a First World one looking in rather than a Third World one looking out. They do not project, in other words, an ethnocentric view of the "native" reality of Latin America.

What is required now, she believes, is a different model or perspective. Juan Loveluck wrote recently that Latin American writers from this point forward will be judged above and beyond their formal and stylistic conquests. They will be judged on their efforts to "decolonize our fiction and make it less dependent on foreign models and standards."[69] Gustav Segade has argued that writers, if they are to be humanistic, must turn to native Americans and recognize in them a link to the *pueblo*, to the new American voice.[70] The *neoindigenismo* of José María Arguedas carried *indigenista* literature and the new humanism in Latin America closer to authenticity, but Arguedas fell short, he seemed to have concluded, because of the impossibility of writing from within. Arguedas realized, perhaps, that total identification, even composing in Quechua, was not enough, for example, to bring about or create an authentic Indian literature, which in the final analysis must come from the Indians themselves.

This realization also applies to literature written by blacks in Latin America. Antonio Cornejo Polar[71] has recognized the heterogeneous nature of Latin American literature, and he significantly extends his theory of heterogeneity in passing to other cultures, namely, those derived from Africa and from the *gaucho* tradition. His main concerns, however, are the Indian and the plural or at least dual nature of Latin American culture. Ethnic variables, he argues, characterize Latin American literature, which makes it difficult to approach from a European or Eurocentric perspective only. Such variables, he insists, are present wherever "conflicting cultures and societies meet."[72]

Similar questions regarding ethnic variables and cultural diversity have to be raised in connection with the black experience in Latin America. Traces of an ethnocentric or "native" model for literary Americanism are found, in part, in Indian literature, in *indigenista* literature, in the *mundonovista* novel, in the new-world phase of modernism, and in the human poetry of Pablo Neruda and César Vallejo. But they come from black folk up as well, as we see these traces beginning, for example, in the *Afrocriollo* movement in the late 1920s, in Alejo Carpentier's later theory of *lo real maravilloso,* and more recently in Roberto Fernández Retamar's use of the Caliban symbol. Further, black writers in Latin America in general definitely take a position from within the Third World looking out.

Chapter Two

From
Black Folk
Up

Our Europe-lovers should not forget
that . . . in order to arrive at
universality it is necessary to begin
with the elements at hand.

—Carlos Arturo Truque

The Afrocriollo Movement Revisited

The *Afrocriollo* movement was the Harlem Renaissance of Latin America. Few events during the first third of this century shaped modern literary Americanism as much as that movement, which saw the black enter Latin American literature definitively both as subject and as author. As part of a general "return to the roots," ethnic types—*gauchos,* Indians, *mestizos,* mulattoes—became common sights in Latin American literature, but none had the dramatic impact or symbolic significance of the black. Literary Americanism, or the search for an authentic American voice, gained impetus with the *Afrocriollo* movement, and the twentieth-century roots of this search became deeply imbedded, for example, in the Afro-oriented writings of Fernando Ortiz, Alejo Carpentier, Luis Palés Matos, and Nicolás Guillén, four Caribbean authors widely identified with the movement and with some of the polemical or controversial issues surrounding it.

The *Afrocriollo* movement enjoyed a very high profile in the late 1920s, 1930s, and 1940s, especially in Afro-Cubanism (the form it took in Cuba) and in Afro-Antilleanism, a term largely associated with the "black" poetry of Luis Palés Matos and with Puerto Rico. However, I do not believe we have a clear picture of what the movement was or why it happened or even its true significance. In general, we know how the movement developed, namely, superficially and externally on the part of nonblack writers who wrote what has come to be called *negrista* poetry and prose, and in a more deeply committed manner on the part of black authors who wrote what can be called *negritud*, or authentic black, poetry. But what was the movement really and what gave rise to the sudden and intense interest in blackness at that moment in the literary history of Latin America? Even the roles of the most important contributors to the movement have not always been clearly delineated and understood, if we are to judge by the lack of unanimity among literary historians.

To begin with, as a minimum we must acknowledge that the movement had two faces (*negrismo* and *negritud*), understand that there was a clear distinction between the two concepts, and recognize the often paradoxical roles of the movement's leading participants and indeed of the movement itself, which propagated negative images of blacks while at the same time finding something of value in blackness. *Negrismo*, unlike *negritud*, generated a dilettante image because of its close similarity to European negrophilia or the scholarly and artistic interest shown in the black by Leo Frobenius, Pablo Picasso, André Gide, Blaise Cendrars, Igor Stravinsky, and others fascinated, for example, with jazz, black art, and the literature of the Harlem Renaissance. Partly inspired by European and North American interest in primitive art and culture, white *negrista* poets turned to the black world. Indeed, many believe *negrismo* was simply an echo of this *moda europea*. Poetic *negrismo* in Puerto Rico and Cuba did have something in common with the European and North American fashion for the primitive and for African and Afro-American art, music and, literature in the 1920s. The exotic approach in Cuba and Puerto Rico, however, though reflecting fascination with the black presence, was tempered by the ever-threatening reality and proximity of that presence which inspired feelings ranging from racist disgust to envy.

There was fascination with the sights, movements, sounds, and rhythms of the black world, which white authors in Latin America tried to capture in song, ballet, prose, and poetry, but the *Afrocriollo* movement did not owe its existence to Cubism and other European *isms* of the time; nor was it an entirely artistic or literary movement. The *Af-*

rocriollo movement was a crisis-oriented phenomenon in which racial, social, and ethnic forces merged to produce a heightened awareness in Latin America of blacks and blackness. The result of this focus was a movement that had a lasting impact on Latin American literature. European primitivism was rampant, as was the fashion for African and Afro-American art, but the living reality of the black and the necessity of coping with this pervading influence were the motivating forces behind the black's emergence as a literary theme and as a producer of literature.

Afro-Cubanism especially, the prominent interest in the black in Cuban literature of that 1920-to-1940 period, was more than a literary phenomenon. Blacks were in a minority in Cuba, but the explanation for Afro-Cubanism can be sought more in the ethnic and social conditions of the country than in the literary fashion for the primitive emanating from Europe. Much of the movement did have the air of a literary fad, but *Afrocriollismo* arose at that moment in Cuban history in response not simply to the European avant-garde but to political problems at home as well. A pressing and controversial issue at the time was the assimilation of a "large and impoverished black population, the backbone of labor in the sugar industry, into the mainstream of political, social, and cultural life."[1]

On one level the *Afrocriollo* movement in Cuba relates to the Africanist movement's search for a primitivistic utopianism in the early twentieth century, but on another and more immediate level the black presence in Cuba demanded attention because of the widespread presence of racism and racial discrimination and their unsettling effects. Despite miscegenation the black continued visible and would not go away. There had been in recent memory even a race war, often called a black revolt, in Cuba. This social upheaval took place in May 1912 and resulted in the deaths of thousands of blacks. The great influx of black workers from neighboring islands to work the sugar factories in the late nineteenth and early twentieth centuries created considerable black phobia. The presence of this cheap labor was unsettling in a racial and socioeconomic sense because some thought the country would be overrun by blacks. And always lurking in the memory of white Cubans was the example of the

Haitian Revolution because of the role it provided for black liberation struggles everywhere.

The Haitian Revolution (1793–1804) had a direct impact on Cuba. For years the fear existed in that neighboring country that blacks would turn it into a black republic. This fear in the mid–nineteenth century led to a massacre of blacks following "the worst racist incident in Cuban history."[2] This incident, known as the Ladder Conspiracy ("La Conspiración de la Escalera), took place in Cuba in 1844. At that time thousands of blacks were executed under suspicion of planning to free the remaining slaves and take over the country. The Haitian Revolution has been called "the most telling event in the Caribbean since the times of discovery."[3] As a result of this successful revolution blacks everywhere, whatever the language they spoke, were made to feel as though they were "part of history."[4] The Haitian Revolution certainly influenced the Ladder Conspiracy, and with these liberation struggles as role models it was not surprising that history repeated itself in Cuba in 1912 when blacks were again objects of "extreme white racist repression."[5] White Cubans had good reason to remain vigilant, which is why aggressive repression became the rule.

Whites in Cuba kept a watchful eye because the black's passion for liberty, which runs throughout the history of Latin America and was especially strong in the Caribbean, had to give cause for concern. Indeed this passion inspired a watchful respect. Out of what they saw as their own "cultural failure"[6] white writers like Carpentier in Cuba came to convert blacks into cultural heroes in tune with cosmic forces of nature. This guarded respect transcended racist stereotypes and led even such racist authors as Luis Palés Matos, the acknowledged initiator of black poetry in Puerto Rico, to seek positive values in blacks.

Oswald Spengler, the "intellectual apostle of the appearance of the Negro in the artistic hemisphere of Europe,"[7] had cast his spell over Palés Matos, and like Spengler, the Puerto Rican poet saw some value in "primitivism" vis à vis what he called the "decadent" bourgeois culture of the white race, which, his argument went, had cut itself off from its roots. The views of Palés Matos, to be sure, represent "one-dimensional primitivist infantilism"[8] at its most racist, but the Puerto Rican author did at times stand in awe of the majestic force of blackness which he exalted ("Majestad negra") and he did acknowledge racial mixture to be the ethnic trademark of the Antilles ("Ten con ten"). Most importantly Palés Matos saw in blacks a positive counterbalance to the cultural bankruptcy of whites.[9]

Perhaps no one kept a more watchful eye than Fernando Ortiz in Cuba. The *Afrocriollo* movement represented a "newly awakened interest in the Black"[10] on the part of whites, and this Cuban anthropologist took a strong interest in the black and his increasing influence in Cuba. The visible black presence propelled Ortiz into academic research on African culture in order to better understand the black world and the black underworld. Ortiz became interested in African culture, we have been told, "for what it could reveal about crime in Cuba."[11] Ortiz's findings contributed greatly to the *negrista* arm of the *Afrocriollo* movement as his racist views of blacks as "people with primitive mentalities and strong proclivities to lust and violence"[12] influenced many *negrista* poets.

Ortiz's work also influenced *negrista* prose, especially Alejo Carpentier's first novel, *Ecué Yambá O*, which, in a sense, represents Ortiz's theoretical views in practice. Like Luis Palés Matos, Carpentier saw some value in black "primitivism" as a counterforce to what he considered to be the cultural failure of whites. Both came to similar conclusions, but Carpentier also applied Ortiz's theories about the criminal tendencies of blacks. Luis Palés Matos, Fernando Ortiz, and Alejo Carpentier are all controversial figures because of the polemical views they have held about blacks at one time or another. Carpentier's first novel, for example, though delving like Ortiz's work into black culture, is, again like Ortiz's work, thoroughly negative and racist toward blacks. "Carpentier's stand throughout the novel," it has been said, "is that African religion is superstition, and her medicine, mere speculation. Menegildo, the hero, is the quintessence of the black stereotype, strong, sexually competent, simple, and simplistic, imbued with hereditary rhythm."[13]

Franz Fanon once said, I believe, that the white intellectual wishes to attach himself to the people, but instead he often only catches hold of their outer garments. Carpentier seemingly only caught hold of the outer garments of the black Cuban in *Ecué Yambá O,* as he himself has often acknowledged his inability to "get inside" the black culture he tried to depict in his first novel. This novel is often dismissed for this reason and others, among them, that the characters are not "universal" or "human"; that the novel is simply a false, nativistic, documentary exercise written at the height of primitivism; and that the novel simply and perhaps innocently propagates a racist, negative, and stereotyped image of blacks, both Haitian and Cuban.

This last reason undoubtedly contains some validity and perhaps represents the decisive factor in Carpentier's decision to dismiss his first novel as "bad." Carpentier, it seems likely, came to realize the racist nature of his early creation, and that realization, perhaps, rather than artistic or faddish reasons, prompted his reluctance to endorse its later release. Carpentier's admirers, however, have insisted on bringing this novel under the critical microscope and have found enough "good" in it to restore the novel to respectability. Carpentier himself acquiesced and eventually permitted an authorized edition in 1979. And why not, since its racism did not seem to deter its popularity among critics. One critic, for example, even while acknowledging the racist and false image of the black-as-primitive in the novel, still builds an entire critical discussion around Carpentier's use and abuse of such an image.[14]

Alejo Carpentier as a young artist in search of a voice in the 1920s, 1930s, and 1940s, turned, like Luis Palés Matos, to the black world in the Caribbean for themes through which he could express his own vision. Seduced by the attraction of primitivism, Carpentier, like many of the *negrista* poets, viewed blacks with the "detached perspective of the inquisitive phenomenologist."[15] More interested in atavism, ritual, and entertainment than in the black per se, Carpentier during this early part of his "black period" explored black culture for what it could contribute to his own artistic vision. At this early stage in his career Carpentier— despite his view under Fernando Ortiz's influence of the black as a primitive "pawn of biological and economic forces"[16] reduced to elemental acts of sex, lust, violence, and crime—also had begun to see the black as an exploited martyr in the economic and historical sense and as a "cultural hero" because of what he perceived as the black's indifference to bourgeois, especially North American, values. Whites began to appear in Carpentier's works as absurd, degenerate representatives of the failure of Western culture, a view best seen in his second novel, *El reino de este mundo* (1949), which has been called the "apocalyptic staging of Spengler's *The Decline of the West.*"[17]

The aesthetic vision in the prose of the early Carpentier, like that of the poetry of the white *negrista* poets of the *Afrocriollo* movement, was a primitivist vision even when used to find something of value in black culture. On the other hand, *negritud,* the other literary product of the *Afrocriollo* movement, was very different. René Dépestre, the Haitian poet now living in Cuba, has written, very perceptively, that "between *negrismo* and *negritud* there exists every qualitative difference that exists between an ordinary wick and the wick of a stick of dynamite."[18] While *negrismo* perpetuated myths and stereotypes, in *negritud,* he writes, "there is a conscious and deliberate preoccupation with the destruction of the myths and stereotypes" of the black.[19]

Another misconception about the *Afrocriollo* movement is the association of Nicolás Guillén with the *negrista* poets of Afro-Cubanism, when in fact he stood apart from this movement and criticized it for not recognizing that in the black world "all is not drum, macumba, rumba, voudou."[20] With good reason Nicolás Guillén has been called "the authentic voice of Afro-Cuban poetry"[21] because he wrote a different literature with a perspective at variance with that of the *negrista* poets. The nineteenth-century antislavery novels were about slaves and about slavery but not of or by slaves. Like these abolitionist novels *negrista* poetry was about blacks but not for them or directed to them. With Nicolás Guillén, however, there was a difference, and the difference between Nicolás Guillén and the Afro-Cubanism practiced by the white *negrista* poets is the same that exists between *negrismo* and *negritud.*

Nicolás Guillén has been much maligned and misunderstood largely because he has been too often forced into the Afro-Cuban mold of Emilio Ballagas, Alejo Carpentier, and Fernando Ortiz, a *negrista* mold into which he never really fit. Guillén is often taken to task for his early

controversial treatment of blacks, his *mulatez,* and his subsequent recon-
ciliation of race with a socialist society. But we should not forget Guillén
reacted early against the negativism of poetic *negrismo.* Perhaps the primary importance of *negrismo* in Cuba was the effect its negative treatment
of blacks had on Guillén in that it—and Langston Hughes—helped force
him out of his ivory tower of modernist complacency. The *Afrocriollo*
movement had two sides, and Guillén ironically came to deny both.
Guillén eventually denied *negritud* just as he had earlier rejected *negrismo,*
and perhaps both for the same reason: to propagate his own theory of
mulatez.

It has been said that Nicolás Guillén came late to Afro-Cubanism, but
my point here is that he did not come to it at all, certainly not to its *negrista*
side, as he rejected the superficialities associated with it. What Guillén
sought and found lacking in the *Afrocriollo* movement and in Cuban
culture in general was authenticity, and his volume of black poems, first
published in Cuba in April 1930,[22] was a defense not only of the African
legacy in Cuban culture but of the national culture itself, which in his
view should not show just European and white North American influences but African influences as well. Guillén sought authenticity and a
new American voice when he campaigned early in this century for fuller
appreciation of the African roots of literary Americanism in Cuba. Tired
of living "my tragedy of being black"[23] Guillén set out to "conquer"
whites because he knew that "by expressing his blackness it was possible
to arrive at what is Cuban."[24]

The role model Nicolás Guillén provided in the 1930s for literary Americanism was an effective one because his black poems struck several
blows at once. On the formal side, Guillén wanted to bring oral forms into
traditional Spanish poetry in Cuba, in effect, to "make the Spanish ballad
Mulatto," or to "Cubanize it."[25] Guillén wanted to recognize the human
reality of the black Cuban, to strip him of his inferiority complex and to
bring him to center stage; and he wanted to fight prejudice and racial
discrimination between blacks and whites and among blacks themselves.
By giving the black dignity and racial pride, Guillén, in the process, was
able to "lay claim to the only thing left that is really ours."[26] And by

creating a genuine Cuban poetry in his black poetry, often considered "the most important and *Cuban* creative current running throughout our literature,"[27] Guillén moved from black pride to national pride.

The importance of Guillén's decision should not be underestimated. Adept as he was in modernist and traditional Spanish verse forms, Guillén knew the time had come for heroic acts if Cubans were to "throw off the shackles of a servile preoccupation with European culture and values to the detriment of their own creativity."[28] To bring the *son* poem, which is what he called his black poetry, center stage was a daring act because although it was popular as a dance beat, "seeing the *son*, in literature, was not the same as dancing to it."[29] The creation of the *son* poem was a daring act of liberation, as much nationalistic as racial and literary. Even at that early stage in his career, Guillén, as he has done throughout his life, was assessing "the ideological needs of his people."[30] His *son* poems have to be seen as the first step in a nationalization process and cannot be dismissed as a folk stage of his poetry or as mere words written for popular songs.[31]

In trying to give literary form to what he saw as a true American voice, Guillén understood thoroughly the significance of and the need for his *son* poem creations. Reading some of his prose pieces written in the 1930s,[32] we clearly see a defiant author steadfastly defending his artistic choices. We are also treated to a fascinating account of the development of the racial, social, cultural, political, and humanistic principles that inform his poetry. But what is especially significant in these early prose pieces is the relevance Guillén's defense has to the concept of blacks as "defenders of the homeland" and as "preservers or symbols of the national culture," two ideas that have been studied recently in some depth by Stephanie Davis-Lett.[33]

In her essay, Davis-Lett studies the relationship between literary presentations of blacks and the concept of *criollismo*. Defining *criollo* the same way I would define the concept of literary Americanism, namely, as that which is "domestic" or "national" or "authentic" or "authentic Americanism,"[34] Stephanie Davis-Lett sees blacks as "symbols of *criollismo*" because of their roles in Latin American literature as defenders of the homeland and as guardians of national cultures. One of her examples is the novel *Juyungo* (1943), by the Afro-Ecuadorian Adalberto Ortiz. In this novel the defense of Ecuador in its border war with Peru rests largely with soldiers of African descent. Davis-Lett gives Carpentier's *Ecué Yambá O* as another example in which blacks are presented as "something more than an ethnic group in Cuban society; they were, in fact," she says, "the guardians of Cuban (and indeed, Antillean) culture as a whole."[35] Her work also shows how the black in Guillén's poetry is often set against the invasion or the influence of what Guillén has called "foxtrot" culture from the United States. The point of her study is that when the black is represented with a positive image in literature, he is cast not as one who "gives up" or "sells out," but as one often found "fighting to preserve what is local and authentic from some sort of foreign interference."[36]

Nicolás Guillén has always rejected the foreign interference of "foxtrot" culture imported from the United States and the "Yankee peril" associated with it. Literary Americanism for a long time has carried the fear of the "Yankee peril," supplanting an earlier cautionary stance toward Europe. Authors in Cuba especially offset this peril by seeking strength and identity in the black, who seemed untouched and certainly unbowed by the U.S. presence, which is why blacks became cultural heroes at home, especially in the early work of Alejo Carpentier. But Nicolás Guillén had another black hero, Langston Hughes, whose influence the Cuban poet has acknowledged. While Guillén rejected "foxtrot" culture, he did recognize the ethnic significance of Langston Hughes and the Harlem Renaissance and the examples of positive blackness to be derived from them.

The Harlem Renaissance was seen by some as superficial, since it shared in the presentation of the black as *nouvelle vogue,* and to a certain extent it was. It did satisfy the curiosity *negrista* poets had for the exotic, but there was another side as well, and like the Haitian Revolution, the Ladder Conspiracy, and the 1912 black revolt in Cuba, the Harlem Renaissance did raise the racial and social consciousness of blacks everywhere. In Latin America Langston Hughes was the best known of the Harlem Renaissance writers, and he did have an impact on the *Afrocriollo* movement, especially on the early black poetry of Nicolás Guillén.

While the *negrista* poets and intellectuals were finding inspiration in the spirit, culture, and rhythms of black culture, in the superficial side of the Harlem Renaissance, and in the European cult of the primitive, Nicolás Guillén had begun to see and insist on the authenticity of his own literary expression and to understand its racial and its national significance. Guillén had read Spengler's *Decline of the West*, as had everybody else of note, and he realized the book's inherent suggestion for a radical new beginning held some value for Latin American culture. For Guillén and for other *Afrocriollo* authors the black stood at the center of this "new beginning"[37] because he represented a "new spirit"[38] in America where the African legacy was often set against the cultural failures of whites.

The *Afrocriollo* movement provided a point of departure in establishing this radical new beginning, and on a larger scale the black as one of the non-European cultures in Latin America represented something of humanistic value white Europe did not have. During the *Afrocriollo* movement white intellectuals came to admire the culture of the forcefully independent black, and this admiration often transcended the superficial image of the black as criminal and primitive they set out to create. The surface result was often superficiality and picturesqueness, but the positive realities of the black contribution were authenticity and essence, two qualities that helped give new-world culture the originality it enjoyed, for example, in the *son* poems of Nicolás Guillén. The black presence contributed greatly to the "particularly rich mixture of political commitment and aesthetic primitivism that is perhaps the trademark of the bulk of Latin American art in the twentieth century."[39]

The *Afrocriollo* movement had its negative side, but by affirming the human value of blackness, the movement helped broaden the search for identity in Latin American and Caribbean literature. The *Afrocriollo* movement had forerunners, as did the Harlem Renaissance and the *négritude* movement, but during the 1920s, 1930s, and 1940s the black Hispanic for the first time came center stage as author, subject, cultural hero, and as an essential component of new-world culture. From ethnic fear caused by the tragedy of the Cuban black, to superficial fascination, and from there to the incorporation of the black legacy in new-world culture, the *Afrocriollo* movement reveals the lasting impact the African presence made on the literary aesthetics of major and minor writers in Latin America.

To discuss this movement as a literary phenomenon only is to overlook this lasting impact and to disregard the continuing need to address the racial, social, and economic factors that gave rise to the movement in the first place. The *Afrocriollo* movement was more than a response to a literary fad emanating from Europe, though the "decline of the West" and the cult of the primitive in Europe at the time did help give the movement legitimacy. The movement *was* a literary response, but to the increasing visibility of the black in the Caribbean who for reasons that were threatening could no longer be overlooked. Nicolás Guillén felt the tragedy of the black Cuban from below and from within, and while *negrista* authors came to see in the black a source for a new beginning, the early black literature of Nicolás Guillén provides the most authentic insight into the social, historical, and racial events that formed the backdrop for that moment in the literary history of Latin America.

Earlier I said that the *Afrocriollo* movement was the Harlem Renaissance of Latin America, and I meant this both in timing and in ethnic participation. Both flourished at a time when blacks were in vogue in Europe and America. In each movement whites were a force controlling to an extent the black image, for better or—mostly—for worse. Black authors and audiences at the time in Latin America were certainly outnumbered, but at that moment in history the black as subject and the black writer did come forth and command attention. With this exposure the black in Havana as in Harlem became a new and certainly a true American voice both symbolically and in reality. Born at a time of great social concern, *Afrocriollismo* was really one of the first genuinely "American" literary movements in this century in Latin America. In the hands of Nicolás Guillén black poetry helped give Latin America a hint of the humanistic, social, and political preoccupations that were to define not only his own poetry but the later "human" poetry of Pablo Neruda and César Vallejo as well.

The Afro Factor in the Marvelous Real

The search for the American voice continued to involve the black presence in the 1940s and 1950s. The African in America was the focal point, for example, in Carpentier's *El reino de este mundo* (1949), his second novel. The black as author—Nicolás Guillén among them—became more visible during the 1940s, but the African heritage in the New World was also associated with this second novel of Carpentier, which like his first, *Ecué Yambá O,* and other, shorter works of his on black themes gave the black in America high visibility. The *Afrocriollo* movement and its search for a new beginning—primarily in the 1930s—helped free Latin America from dependency on Europe-oriented cultures. In the 1940s Carpentier's version of magic realism outlined in his theory of *lo real maravilloso* continued to focus attention inward.

During the 1940s Carpentier was still looking for his "voice" and for an autonomous and independent mode of expression in the New World, and again he turned his artistic attention to the marvelous reality of the new-world black. The fantastic presence of the black in America fascinated the Cuban author, and events of the Haitian Revolution played a role in the formulation of his theory of the "Marvelous American Reality" which involves seeing reality from "the other side, the side of the Afro-Antillians."[40] In this theory African drums again beat "beneath the surface of Latin American consciousness,"[41] as the African presence in the New World surfaced in the extraordinary personalities and exploits of Macandal, Bouckman, Henri Christophe, and others to help make that world marvelous, bigger than life, and beyond belief—unless, of course, one is a believer. The magical conception of reality is not exclusively limited to those nations with a population of indigenous or African descent, but these ethnic elements are very much present in much of Latin America where the concept of "magic realism," certainly as Carpentier understands it, is especially suited for capturing the essence of life in that part of the world.

Well known is Ray Verzasconi's definition of magical realism, which he gives in big letters: "AN EXPRESSION OF THE NEW WORLD REALITY WHICH AT ONCE COMBINES RATIONAL ELEMENTS OF THE EUROPEAN SUPER-CIVILIZA-

TION AND IRRATIONAL ELEMENTS OF A PRIMITIVE AMERICA."[42] This definition, as Verzasconi applies it to the works of Miguel Angel Asturias, sees
the European super-civilization as Carpentier saw it, namely, more decadent and sordid than "primitive America." Verzasconi, through Asturias's work and in the Guatemalan's use of myth and superstition,
explores the telluric roots of American man. James Irish, like Verzasconi,
sees the term *magic realism* in its ethnocentric context as best describing
the search for Caribbean and Latin American roots.[43] Irish links magic
realism to African-descended populations of Latin America and to the
Latin Americans' desire to understand themselves and the originality of
their literature and national identities. He links the term to the examina-
tion Latin Americans have made of their human types, local scenes, and
traditional speech forms over the years. The awareness of human types,
Irish argues, moves beyond the exotic, even beyond social and economic problems, to initiate a reevaluation of indigenous and black values. Magic realism represents, he contends, the fulfillment of a search
for root-qualities—African roots, Indian roots, ethnic roots—underly-
ing the regional experience. Magic realism and *Afrocriollismo* should be
considered as more than literary phenomena because both terms relate
to and derive from attempts to define the essence of Latin American
identity based on that which is of value locally.

Irish recognizes the wider interpretation of the term *magic realism*,
which apparently was invented by the German critic Franz Roh in 1925,
but he rejects Angel Flores's argument that all magical realists create
ambiguity and confusion and cater not to popular taste but to an exclusive literary elite. Flores errs further, Irish insists, in using Borges to
illustrate the term. Borges may be "an artisan in his use of language and
an alchemist of fantastic reality,"[44] but his esoteric world, Irish claims, is
hardly in touch with the *esencias* of Latin America as more down-to-
earth interpreters see them. Irish dismisses Borges's kind of magic realism: "His magic realism is a contrived atmosphere of complexity, confusion, and fancy created by his stylistic devices."[45]

"Created by his stylistic devices" is the key phrase here because other
interpreters of magic realism—Miguel Angel Asturias, Gabriel García
Máquez, and Alejo Carpentier among them—stand in diametrical op-

position to Borges's magic realism since they anchor the term in the "natural roots" found in surrounding reality. To them, Irish has argued, magic reality comes before technique and style in that it is not the result of stylistic devices but rather the essence and matter for which forms of expression have to be found. We are cautioned to remember, for example, that García Márquez considers himself a realist writer even, or especially, when he is writing about fantastic and extraordinary things because what he is actually doing is transcribing events that are "real" in Latin America.

Similar points have been made about Asturias and about Carpentier, whose own phrase applies to the authentic—not contrived—reality he sees in Latin America. For Carpentier events are more marvelous than magical; they are marvelous and strange, but real and not supernatural. The truth of *lo real maravilloso* is stranger than the creative fiction of verbal invention. Carpentier expresses "utter contempt for writers who create fantastic worlds that have no bearing on their personal experience."[46] In doing this, he updates the search for "the real American essences" and for literary Americanism by insisting on authenticity in a term that purports to express what is original in the New World. Carpentier particularly has been very insistent on full recognition for the African legacy in the new-world reality, as the black, like the Indian, helps form the ethnic core of the "peculiar style of life in America."[47] With his focus on the African in America, Carpentier's theory of *lo real maravilloso* represents, in a sense, a continuation of the *Afrocriollo* movement, as both are affirmations not only of the black experience in the New World but of the ongoing search for the true American voice.

Carpentier was crucial in the *Afrocriollo* roots of literary Americanism in the 1920s and the 1930s. The presence of the black in his work continued to be crucial, and polemical too. But despite the controversial nature of the black image in his first two novels, Carpentier has appreciated the significance of the black presence in his search for something authentic and exclusively Latin American. Like Luis Palés Matos, Nicolás Guillén, and others, Carpentier had read Spengler's *Decline of the West*, and in his ethnocentric, or Afrocentric, view of the world in Haiti, Cuba, and the Caribbean, whites and Europeans fare badly. The Cuban author went from black folk up in his approach to Latin American culture. His experiences with surrealism might have taught him how to see, but what he saw was real, human, and marvelous, not invented.

*Afro-*mestizaje *and* Calibán

Roberto Fernández Retamar's position in *Calibán* (1971),[48] like Carpentier's theory of *lo real maravilloso* and the earlier *Afrocriollo* movement, is another move from black folk up, where white intellectuals in this century look to the example of nonwhite masses in Latin America. Fernández Retamar's book is important because of the Afro focus it gives to the new response discussed in the previous chapter and to *mestizaje,* the one element in Latin American culture, literature, and society that has overshadowed most others.

The Cuban author argues in favor of both recognition for the nonwhite *contexto* of Latin American societies and complete identification with it—an identification, he suggests, the *mestizo* nature of these societies makes inevitable. To Fernández Retamar "marginal" elements—the people and their forms of expression—should move to center stage, and he supports the need to highlight the originality of the black, Indian, and *mestizo* contributions in Latin America. He goes beyond that need, however, by seeking total ethnic identification with Third World peoples and by respecting works by them.

This total identification through *mestizaje* that lies at the core of Fernández Retamar's approach to Latin America becomes an indispensable clue in the search for the "unifying formula," the *centro de cohesión interior,* of Latin American literature. The assumption here is that there can be no authentic concept of literary Americanism that excludes the *mestizo* reality of what some refer to as the *"mestizo* continent." *Mestizaje,* through cultural and racial symbiosis, deepens and broadens nationalism "beyond the framework established by European and Occidental civilization."[49] Even stronger than *indigenismo, africanismo,* and *hispanidad,* which some see as devisive concepts, *mestizaje,* in Fernández Retamar's view, is a better embodiment of *la especificidad latinoamericana,* which is why he makes it a key concept in the cultural and intellectual declaration of independence his *Calibán* represents.

Intellectuals in Latin America, he insists, should identify with Calibán (the slave). The "slave," represented by oppressed and exploited peoples of the Third World, is now symbolized by Shakespeare's Caliban who carries that role nicely in the twentieth century. Fernández Retamar's Third World vision lays great stress on nonwhite victims of "imperialism." This vision, which makes his identification with cultural and ethnic *mestizaje* in Latin America very political, assures a native or original approach to the continent's history, culture, and literature. In his view Calibán must become the new Latin American protagonist, as he best reflects the human reality of that area, whose history, culture, and literature must be told through the example of this *mestizo* "native" protagonist and not from the point of view of the "enslaver." Fernández Retamar's vision of Latin America not only rejects recent writers "blinded" by European and occidental models; the Cuban author's objection goes all the way back to Sarmiento, whom he sees as one of the first to downgrade *mestizaje* which, Fernández Retamar insists, should be seen not as "sickness" but as positive symbol.

Again, from black folk up comes the true American voice. There is more honor, Fernández Retamar has argued, to be considered descendants of the rebellious African slave than of the enslaver. It no longer is a question of speaking magnanimously about blacks or about Indians. We must speak, he has insisted, as blacks, as Indians, and as the cultural and racial *mestizos* that we are. *Calibán* is a strongly political book, but it is at the same time a special kind of *concientización* (consciousness raising) in that it puts as much faith in *mestizaje* as in class. *Calibán* deals with national identities, but more than just racial and cultural mixing the work signals a symbolic reversal of identity roles where those down under become the real heroes. Fernández Retamar's use of *mestizaje* is similar to that found in two Venezuelan novels—Rómulo Gallegos's *Pobre negro* (1937) and Ramón Díaz Sánchez's *Cumboto* (1950)—and in Francisco Arriví's *Vejigantes* (1956), a play about race in Puerto Rico. There is in these works, as in Fernández Retamar's *Calibán*, a complete turnabout from Sarmiento's nineteenth-century blatant racism, which reflected the belief that a racially mixed population contributed more to *la barbarie* than to *la civilización.*

The *Afrocriollo* writers showed interest in the black partly for what he had to offer of human value and also because of what white society had failed to deliver, namely, a positive image. In the same vein, whites appear in a negative light in Carpentier's *El reino de este mundo* and in other novels as well: Arturo Uslar Pietri's *Las lanzas coloradas* (1931) and Ramón Díaz Sánchez's *Cumboto,* to name only two. Mulattoes, on the other hand, were often presented as the race of the future. For some the black laid the foundation for a new beginning, but for others the mulatto became the ideal representative of the new American man—certainly in the Caribbean where the works of such different authors as Luis Palés Matos and Nicolás Guillén shared the same vision of the area's ethnic future. Fernández Retamar's *Calibán* recalls earlier works that extolled *mestizaje* and is, in a sense, a return to and an update of the message they contained. The significance of his position, however, is its rejection of the belief that white is always good and nonwhite bad, savage, and barbaric. The kind of thinking the Cuban intellectual supports gives respectability to ethnic peoples in America in the continuing search for authentic new-world models.

If we extend our discussion to Brazil we will find that Abdias do Nascimento, perhaps the best-known black Brazilian writing today, for a long time has voiced a similar need for his countrymen to recognize the contribution of Afro-Brazilians to authentic Brazilian culture. To Nascimento the road to what is genuinely Brazilian is again, as in Spanish America, from black folk up. Nascimento, considered Brazil's leading black playwright, has insisted since 1944, when he founded the Teatro Experimental do Negro (TEN), that "official" Brazilian culture is not Brazilian but imitation European culture. The "real" Brazilian, or the "genuinely" Brazilian, he says, must be found in the world of the folk, which to him is essentially Afro-Brazilian. Nascimento has given preeminence to Afro-Brazilian folk culture in such works as *Sortilégio* (1951). This attempt to bring authenticity to the Brazilian theater ran into censorship problems, and the play's staging was delayed until 1957.[50]

Chapter Three

Modern
Black
Heroism

My heroes . . . moved through the world with a bit of their humanism still intact.

—Don Lee

In the continuing search for authentic new-world models, we can turn with interest to Adalberto Ortiz's novel *Juyungo* (1943) and to its black hero-protagonist Ascención Lastre, or Juyungo. While many black writers in Latin America portray the black as heroic defender, representative, and guardian of national cultures, black heroism is singularly apparent in Ortiz's important black Ecuadorian novel, as it has been throughout the black experience in the New World. Black heroism takes many forms in history and in literature. Heroic black rebels both slave and free are legendary, for example, in Latin America where heroic acts of exemplary black figures range from epic militancy to a defiance with words. The art of survival in whatever form is a heroic art—as is the telling of it—for the underdog, and the black has been that. Any black figure who presents a positive model is a hero whether he is acting on behalf of his people, on his own behalf, or in the name of country.

The black is a new-world symbol of *criollismo*. His role as guardian of national culture and as defender of homelands, however, dates back in part to Spain, whose early history and literature include black heroes who acted on behalf of the Spanish nation and the Catholic religion. Four works where the black hero appears in seventeenth-century Spanish drama as scholar, soldier, saint, and noble are Diego Ximénez de Enciso's *La comedia famosa de Juan Latino,* Andrés de Claramonte's *El valiente negro de Flandes,* Lope de Vega's *El Santo negro Rosambuco,* and Luis Véjez de Guevara's *Virtudes vencen señales,* respectively.[1] But blacks like Juan Latino who were presented as heroes not only had to adopt Christianity and express Spanish values and the Spanish way of life; they also had to pay a price, namely, "cut loose"[2] from their African origins.

Black heroes in early Spain were really "Spanish gentlemen" in a Spanish society that allowed them to be heroes when their *raison d'être* was Spain, when they functioned outside of their ethnic background.[3] Like other Spaniards they had to struggle against "villainous Jews and Moors"[4] who opposed Christianity and who tried to take over economically and politically. Unlike the Jew and the Moor the black was not a threat, which is why he could be a Spanish hero expressing Spanish—not black—values. Early black heroes wanted "to move up the social ladder in Spain,"[5] but before black slavery—that is, before the discovery and colonization of the New World—blacks in Spain were caught up in some bloody religious wars.

In the New World, blacks continued to be heroes as explorers, soldiers, and maroon rebels, to name only three potentially heroic occupations. There is much heroism in the black experience in America, whether it took the form of slave insurrection or opposition to Spain. In the New World, black heroes were not fighting the enemies of Spain but the Spanish themselves, and Creoles too. In other words, blacks were now fighting whites, and such rebel leaders as El rey Miguel in Venezuela, El rey Bayano in Panama, Zumbi of Palmares, and Felipillo in Panama epitomized the true black hero in the New World because they established their own *raison d'être:* they were not interested in satisfying white society.

Many of these heroes and others like them were immortalized in literature. Black writers themselves, from slavery times to the present, overcame hardships and faced life heroically and creatively. Black heroic figures appear in such twentieth-century novels as Juan Pablo Sojo's *Nochebuena negra,* Adalberto Ortiz's *Juyungo,* Nelson Estupiñán Bass's *Senderos brillantes,* Quince Duncan's *La paz del pueblo,* Manuel Zapata Olivella's *Chambacú* and *Changó, el gran putas,* and Carlos Guillermo Wilson's *Chombo.* Natividad, the narrator-protagonist of Ramón Díaz Sánchez's *Cumboto,* represents to some "an emerging hero: the black intellectual."[6] But whether the black hero is "cerebral," a redeemer figure, or a social activist, he must meet, to an extent, modern black criteria. Unlike the black heroes used by white writers to symbolize nation, religion, or national culture, true black heroes today are idolized by blacks because like the maroon heroes of old, they represent heroic insistence on their own societal values rather than somebody else's.

A true black hero who is heroic to his people is often antiheroic to some whites, especially when it is against their social values that he rebels. Heroism for blacks

has always meant some measure of revolt against social structures, for these structures were the instruments of their oppression rather than their protection . . . In order to find a Black version of a hero, one must look someplace other than the definitions proffered by Western traditions. One can find him in the character types who are immortalized in Black songs and legends, in Black fact and reality. He is the rebel leader who revolts against physical bondage, and the streetman, the hard man . . . Black people will applaud, admire and envy these heroes.[7]

It has been said that a true black hero in the eyes of black people is more likely to be a lawbreaker than a lawmaker.[8] Martin Luther King, Jr., we all remember, stood on the side of justice even when that stance set him against unjust laws of white society.

Blacks are presented in literature as heroes or redeemers of national communities, but the heroic motivation is largely symbolic of a national rather than a black identity. Blacks do possess qualities that make them ideal symbols for positive models, but some white writers in Latin America as in early Spain present a positive image of the black as hero only when he is fighting against someone else, like Spanish loyalists or foreign invaders. Salvador Golomon, the "brave Black" in Silvestre de Balboa's *Espejo de paciencia* (1608) can be a "national hero" because he defeats a French pirate who was attacking Cuba. He is not a "black hero" in the maroon tradition, for example, of Zumbi of Palmares or of Gabriel de la Concepción Valdés ("Plácido"). "Plácido," Cuba's heroic black poet, was a perfect black hero because during slavery times in colonial Cuba he was suspected of plotting against Spaniards *and* Creoles, which means he had no chance at all and he was shot, executed on suspicion.

A Model Black Hero

Ascensión Lastre, or Juyungo, the black protagonist of Adalberto Ortiz's novel *Juyungo*, is another perfect black hero, one for our time. Elsewhere I have called this novel a black Ecuadorian classic[9] largely because it is saturated with blackness in form, character, and theme. In *Juyungo*, Ascensión, like Golomon, fights against foreign invaders, but we have come a long way from the black as warrior-soldier in America fighting in wars of independence or against French pirates. Ascensión Lastre is a heroic rebel, even an outlaw, in the eyes of "white society." In the maroon tradition he stood firm against unjust authority. Like rebel heroes before him Juyungo's main motivation was to prove his worth.

Ascensión Lastre was a restless black who yearned to do something worthy and heroic. In a sense he lived by the law of the jungle, where man has to choose in an instant among killing, being killed, or being considered a coward. And Lastre, "like many Blacks, is rightly proud of being no weakling."[10] Nothing aroused his emotions so much as tales of heroism, especially about the Conchist Rebellion, which took place in the Ecuadorian province of Esmeraldas in 1912, the same year as the black revolt in Cuba. This rebellion, to Ascensión, was "nothing more than the retaliation of his race, oppressed and humiliated for centuries" (p. 38). Commandant Lastre, Ascensión's uncle, fought in that war, and he is indeed the heroic example his nephew strives to emulate. We never see his uncle in action, but the heroic exploits of this famous relative provide the guiding force behind Ascensión's own code of behavior. Even going to war, as we shall see, was more an act of imitation than of patriotism. Ascensión, like his uncle, was a *macho* man, a black *macho* man. Black heroism is synonymous with black *machismo* in this novel where one must act like a man, take pain like a man, and toughen up like a man. A courageous black who "did not cry even when tears flowed against his will" (p. 185), Ascensión lived up to the saying "Real men do not die in bed." As he goes through life "fighting like real men do,"[11] Ascensión, like his uncle before him, becomes a classic black hero even though to white society he, again like his uncle, was considered to be "bad, through and through."[12] Ascensión was a man of feeling, but "hardened by the temper of life" (p. 174) he retaliated and killed in the name of avenging justice. Like his uncle, Ascensión was, to whites, guilty of committing horrendous crimes.

But to blacks the phrase "What a man your uncle was! the famous Commandant Lastre" sums up his uncle's positive image. Likewise Ascensión was considered a "savage" to whites, but to blacks he was a true black hero, "a remarkable man, a Black with a noble soul who wasn't born to be a slave, one who would die if necessary fighting for his freedom" (p. 71). Commandant Lastre, like Zumbi of Palmares, was an irritant to white society, but not to blacks. Like Ascensión, those men were heroes in the eyes of blacks since they epitomized the black hero who opposed forces aligned against them. One man's hero is another man's outlaw. Ascensión's aggressiveness against injustice is dismissed as "foul-tempered," but not by those on whose side he fought. "Justice" to Ascensión meant the murders he committed, not "white" society holding him criminally responsible or accountable for them.

Ascensión killed two men who were symbols of the forces of oppression. Blacks in the novel felt satisfaction on learning of his deed, and Ascensión, for his part, knew none of them would tell anyone anything about his "criminal act" (p. 183). Ascensión was a man of action who set an example by what he did. His few but well-chosen words displayed a heroic determination that would never allow prejudice, personal tragedy, or injustice to get him down. "I am a Lastre!" he would emphasize, and when justifying resistance he would say, "That's what men are for!"

Ascensión Lastre was a model black hero who gained heroic stature in the eyes of other blacks because of his physical strength and his courage. He was a fighter, but despite his hardness he was capable of tenderness and compassion, and he was no fool. Ascensión was an expert at recognizing sham and rejected fraud of all kinds whether practiced by the Catholic church or by witch doctors. He did not fall for supernatural stories, superstition, or religious hypocrites, nor was he deceived by the lies of his exploiters.

Though a hard man, Ascensión was a good man in the eyes of other blacks. He knew the difference between right and wrong, and he instinctively spoke out and reacted in favor of the right. To be a black hero it is not enough to be big and strong. Cocambo, the black antagonist in the novel, was big and strong, but he was also servile to whites. Unlike Juyungo, Cocambo used his strength against blacks and in the employ of whites. Cocambo matched Ascensión in strength and massive physique but he was a "black bully" scorned "for being servile and groveling before the bosses and because he treated others . . . as if he were white" (p. 67). The battle that had been smoldering throughout the novel between Cocambo and Ascensión, the "two ebony giants," was more than a fight: it was a heroic confrontation between good and evil. In this battle Ascensión was fighting the person he held responsible for the death of his son. His rage was fueled, however, by his hatred of the kind of corrupt, servile black that Cocambo represented, whom he disliked even more than corrupt, racist whites who exploited blacks simply because of their color. Ascensión is a true black hero because he is proud of his color; at no time does he wish to be white or to enter the white man's world.

In one sense one can easily contrast Ascensión Lastre with José Pastrana, the black protagonist of *El último río* (1966), by Ortiz's Afro-Ecuadorian compatriot Nelson Estupiñán Bass. Pastrana started out like Ascensión, believing himself to be a "negro fuerte," a "strong black," but he soon changes and becomes an antiblack social climber. For a while Pastrana is an antihero, a "white puppet" who obtains the support of whites but the wrath of blacks. Pastrana reacts aggressively in his displays of black *machismo*, but not in the same way as Ascensión, who unlike Pastrana never took advantage of other blacks. Blacks felt admiration for Ascensión, whose heroic feats even included killing a lion with a machete.

Blacks also felt admiration for Nelson Díaz, another important character to the black community in Ortiz's novel. Although Jonathan Tittler considers Nelson Díaz a replica of the educated exploiter,[13] this almost white "intellectual" character in the novel can be considered a hero in his own right. Black characters admire him and Ascensión does not want him to change, even though Nelson himself would like to be more black. Nelson Díaz qualifies as an intellectual hero, one who speaks his mind. Nelson has a reasoning approach to everything. He does not hate all whites, only those who are enemies of the people. Ascensión eventually gets this message and he does learn to temper his own hatred of whites. Nelson and Ascensión had spent time in prison and both had committed heroic acts on behalf of justice. In his own way Nelson was a tough man who lived the strength of his convictions. His belief that it is essential to be a man and to confront life with a dignified and courageous attitude sums up not only his own intellectual analysis of life but Ascensión's instinctive behavior as well.

As heroes, Nelson and Ascensión are sensitive to prejudice and to the misfortunes of others. They react in different ways but they do react. What impresses most about Ascensión is his heroic defense of his and others' blackness. He would stand no jokes or insults, for example, at his own expense or that of the black community. In addition, knowing what it is like to be an underdog, Ascensión was quick to come to the defense of other underdogs of any color. Just as he defended blacks from insulting jokes, so too does he come to the aid of the white character Valerio who was outnumbered in a fight with the police, and he saved a terrified Indian girl of eleven from a rape attempt by the antagonist Cocambo.

Extreme confidence in his own abilities stands out among Ascensión's character traits and coalesces perfectly with his pride in blackness and his constant affirmation of his black identity. Ascensión seems to have been born with black self-awareness, and he is consistent throughout the novel. Even when he lived among the Cayapa Indians he affirmed his black identity by refusing to coat his body with a reddish substance used by his hosts. We never lose sight of Ascensión's individual black consciousness even when he tries, on Nelson's advice, to see beyond race. With Ascensión we always have one black's individual response to victimization. With a heroic black uncle as his model Ascensión always strives to be a black hero himself. This is true even when he goes to war.

Ascensión hails from Esmeraldas, the black province of Ecuador, and this place of origin is significant in the development of his heroic status both in peace and in wartime. The black Esmeraldan *macheteros* were known for their bravery. Such reputations were established by earlier Esmeraldan blacks like Commandant Lastre, and subsequent black generations had to uphold them. Ascensión epitomized the heroism black Esmeraldans were known for, and this regional affiliation colors even the national orientation the author tries to give his novel in the final pages. *Juyungo* can be considered a national novel, but its trajectory, originating from the individual, travels through the racial and regional.

Ascensión, brave like his warrior uncle, went to war against the Peruvians voluntarily, to display his valor and his strength. He went to war "not for the fatherland *but for himself;* he was also the fatherland."[14] Going to war was an act of pride in being from the black province of Esmeraldas. *Juyungo* shows that blacks have qualities the larger Ecuadorian society would like to be known for, like bravery. Stretching the truth, one character in the novel wishfully states, "You Esmeraldans always had a reputation for bravery, *like all Ecuadorians*" (p. 195), a statement that belies the absence of whites at the front lines. When the fighting became fierce only blacks and Indians stood their ground, while the officers, all of them, retreated to the rear guard.

The black Esmeraldans were, in a sense, trapped by their own reputations. Known as good fighters, they had to fulfill their obligation to fight; their fighting reputation really left them no alternative but to go to war. This personal, racial, and regional obligation, then, should not be confused with patriotism. The blacks from Esmeraldas were, to be sure, "the first contribution of blood from an abandoned province to the cause of national sovereignty" (p. 199). Ortiz's black characters, however, are defending Ecuador because of a pride in self the country should but does not have and depends on them to exhibit.

The war scenes at the end of the novel are more of a condemnation of Ecuador than of enemy Peru. Ortiz criticizes his country for sending troops to the front lines poorly equipped and poorly supported and for abandoning them to their own bravery with no doctors, officers, weapons, or supplies. Again, other Ecuadorians should be more like the black Ecuadorians and not like those who sent them there. At any rate, Ascensión, "the magnificent Black," died in this war never betraying to the very end his reputation as "a brave black man," one who with unlimited confidence went to war "to commit a feat worthy of a Lastre, of a Black's Black" (p. 208). Even in a national war it came down to a "handful of Blacks, determined to give it their all" (p. 211).

Ascensión Lastre gave it his all in one final act of black *macho* bravura. Pinned down by the enemy, short of supplies and hungry, Ascensión decided to make a heroic one-man foray under the cover of darkness into enemy territory to steal food. Taking off his clothes so that his black body would blend in with the night and armed only with a machete, he told his friend, "light a fire . . . tonight we eat" (p. 208). Ascensión set out confidently and succeeded in infiltrating an enemy machine-gun position and in stealing food. He tried to fight his way out and "with a feeling of overflowing strength" (p. 209) fought bravely and fiercely against great odds. But the task he had set for himself was an impossible one and he was killed. It is perhaps easy to see this final act of heroism as suicidal or as the action of a man insane. But it was, simply, one more act of courage, the last one Ascensión committed: he died trying to get food for himself and for his fellow soldiers starving in the trenches.

Juyungo as Mythical Figure, Archetype, and Symbol

Ascensión has been called the "universal Latin American black man"[15] because his life was no different from that of other blacks who suffer the same kinds of racist insults that define the black experience in Latin America. In addition to his heroic significance for blacks, Ascensión represents the standard quest of the hero whose exemplary life becomes a voyage to consciousness: Ascensión journeys out as an adolescent, overcomes hostile forces, and survives into manhood, and he thus conforms, as Martha Cobb has observed, "to the traditional outlines of a hero figure to be found in all cultures."[16] Ortiz, Cobb believes, was looking at his black protagonist in two ways: as an ideal black hero figure who will prove to be a "savior" or "redeemer" of his race, and as the archetypal raceless being who will transcend race.[17]

Ronna Newman,[18] Ortiz's biographer, looks at Juyungo as a black hero, a mythic character, and as an archetypal figure. As a black hero he is seen by both Cobb and Newman as fulfilling the role of "redeemer" or "savior." As a mythic character Ascensión is defined by Newman as a primordial being, an elemental force of nature, whose death is the sacrifice necessary for the regeneration and renewal of life. In this sense Ascensión becomes a symbol of the eternal return. Further, a rampaging river in the novel represents the torrent within that causes Ascensión to erupt. More than just a river, the rampaging waters symbolize the boundless energy and violent anger of Ascensión, who is indeed called a "boundless force of the tropics." But like the river, this potent, surging torrent of fury can also be calm.

As an archetypal hero Ascensión becomes a raceless redeemer, a heroic figure who dies a heroic death. In this characterization Newman considers Ascensión a universal being who opposes the forces of evil. According to her concept,

the exceptionally strong and brave hero departs from the known world and journeys to the so-called center of the universe, the 'world navel'. Here the hero encounters the sources of good and evil and of beauty and ugliness. He successfully undergoes initiatory trials, triumphing over malevolent forces. After having experienced a sense of unity between himself and the divinity, he returns to the world bringing a boon for mankind. His final stage is characterized by his fallibility to the sin of pride (hubris) and his fall through betrayal or a heroic sacrifice that ends in his death.[19]

Ascensión could fit this description: his black pride does spur him to sacrifice self for the good of others. He certainly journeys out, encounters good and evil, triumphs over evil, and dies through excessive confidence. On a mythical and archetypal level Ascensión is elevated "above the occasional and the transitory into the sphere of the everexisting".[20] This universalization of his struggle to remain free, according to Newman, makes the contemporary reader respond more intensely to Ascensión's story. In making this assertion, Newman, at the same time, insists that the Marxist ideology which Ascensión struggles to understand flaws the total portrait of Lastre as a mythical symbol.

While there might be some conflict between myth and modern ideology in the novel, there is little that would detract from the positive black presence Ascensión represents. He does not consciously strive to be a "savior" or "redeemer" of his race or of humanity. Yet Ascensión is a model black hero because he instinctively rejects, as we all should, wrongdoing. The author tells us that Ascensión seems to be a "symbol of his race in motion, growing and growing."[21] Our hero almost intuitively searches for "freedom's road," and we see this heroic quest in his constant confrontation with insult, injustice, and exploitation. Myth, symbol, or archetype notwithstanding, it is easy to see in Ascensión Lastre "an epic hero representing the black cause . . . the embodiment of all that is noble in his people."[22]

Ascensión Lastre embodies a heroic quest for betterment of self and of others like him. On an individual level his rebellious or maroon spirit was his way out even when it set him against overwhelming odds. Marisol Ballester[23] sees this individual revolutionary alternative doomed to failure and, like Nelson Díaz and Ortiz himself, would choose collective revolution, a class alternative that would change whole systems and structures rather than individuals. Overriding the larger alternatives, however, is a necessary first ingredient not only for black writers but for black heroes and heroines in literature as well, namely, an acceptance of self that enables one to meet life "head on" and with dignity.

There is something to be said for the "loneliness and heroism of individualized revolt."[24] Meeting life "head on" is a prerequisite to physical liberation, as one must free the individual spirit first. Richard Wright never relinquished his belief in the necessity for individual action as a prerequisite for freedom even when he flirted with collectivism in the late 1930s by joining the Communist party.[25] Richard Wright supported the dignity of "the sheer brute man, just as he is."[26] Ascensión has this same dignity, and this basic quality makes him a black literary hero or model worth emulating.

The Human Meaning of Juyungo

Juyungo, Ortiz's "sheer brute man," is a model black hero who shows us how to live and die with dignity. In the arena of image Ortiz's black protagonist stands out as an unforgettable literary creation. By depicting this Afro-Esmeraldan world with its black heroes, Ortiz has participated in the ongoing "quest for the essence of the American continent."[27] Like other black writers in Latin America he is writing in the tradition of literary Americanism. Although Ortiz replaces "the conventional white model for action with a black one,"[28] his Ascensión Lastre is as legitimate a new-world literary hero as such folk types as the Argentine *gaucho* and the American cowboy. This black model is an American model, and Ascensión's heroes are not African kings, though they would have been had he known of them. But since he knew nothing of Africa his heroes were, like himself, black *macho* Americans from Esmeraldas.

In his own way Ascensión Lastre is a true American voice whose indomitable spirit becomes contagious. The human values he seeks— justice, brotherhood, and freedom—are the same ones he sacrificed his life for. His concern for his own dignity and that of others like him took precedence over all else, and the here and now took precedence over an afterlife; in *Juyungo* human struggles are not displaced "to a celestial plane."[29] Whether understood on a racial, national, or universal level the human meaning of *Juyungo* is clear; the novel "is not an example of the cryptic 'dehumanized' art Ortega y Gasset saw looming on the horizon of the 1920s."[30] Rather it is an admirable and effective example of the humanist legacy of black Hispanic literature. It is, as well, like the *Afrocriollo* movement, an early example of the quest for ethnic authenticity in the literature of the area.[31]

Chapter Four

The
Great New
Mandinga

*White people cannot in the generality
be taken as models of how to live.*

—James Baldwin

*Paint yourselves black and become
Mulattoes, workers, peasants and
step down to the people.*

—Ché Guevara

"Paint Yourselves Black"

Ché Guevara's symbolic advice to intellectuals and revolutionaries in Latin America to "paint yourselves black" recognizes, despite opposition to it,[1] an important point, namely, that the black Latin American provides a role model in the search for authenticity and the American voice. Blacks are more than subjects and authors; they are *defenders* of their homelands, *guardians* of national cultures, and *representatives* of these homelands and cultures as well. Recognition of this role model came from *mundonovista* and *Afrocriollista* authors. Carpentier advanced a similar notion through his theory of *lo real maravilloso*, as did Fernández Retamar more recently with his focus on Caliban and in his extolling of *mestizaje*.

Afro-Hispanic literature, like Ortiz's *Juyungo* and Guillén's *son* poems, supports the claim for a heterogeneous literary Americanism. There is a corpus of such literature written in Spanish by "realistically committed" black authors. Since this black literature is written "from within" it provides a more authentic image, certainly, of black life than the literary expression of " 'concerned' white humanists"[2] who, despite their advocacy, remain on the outside looking in. Inauthenticity was one of the major criticisms leveled even against the "old masters": while their focus was American ethnic reality, they still were writing about other peoples' lived experiences. Carpentier's criticism of his own novel *Ecué Yambá O*, for example, is well known, perhaps more so than the novel itself. Accusations of inauthenticity, however, can hardly be leveled at the literature of Candelario Obeso, Nicolás Guillén, Adalberto Ortiz, and Juan Pablo Sojo, four representative black authors whose expressions of literary Americanism grow out of their own lived experiences. The sense of honest identification blacks bring to black writing is a necessary prerequisite for any truly authentic expression of the African heritage.[3] When that heritage is understood in its new-world context it becomes evident that black literature can represent literary Americanism at its most genuine.

In addition, parallels can be established between the black experience and the larger Latin American experience. The search for identity, for example, is an important parallel, especially regarding the issue of duality where blacks and Latin Americans have had to shed the same "Mask of the Metropolis" Fanon spoke of when he talked of blacks "hankering for assimilation."[4] H. Hoetink underscored another significant parallel when he wrote, "While it is true that the collective feelings of the Negroes' dignity have been corroded by their much-remembered slavery past, by their present generally low status, and . . . by their recent colonial past . . . such humiliating feelings are shared by the Indians and by Indo-America generally."[5] It is possible to look at differences, for example, between indigenism and negritude, or between Indo– and Afro–Spanish America, but it is more profitable to seek similarities between the black and Indian experiences and make them serve as the basis for a new interpretation of the history, culture, and literature of the larger Latin American society.

Leopoldo Zea[6] sees *négritude* and *indigenismo* as new-world reactions to dependency, but from the outset he makes one important distinction: he recognizes that negritude, unlike indigenousness, arises from within the black man himself and not from well-meaning but nonblack authors. Both were formed, however, out of a marginality created by assumptions of racial and cultural superiority emanating from Europe and from people with European backgrounds. Latin America had the same problem, Zea argues, particularly after independence when Latin Americans had to reject the colonial mentality that had imposed an inferiority complex on the former colonies. Both blacks and Latin Americans had to question, as Fernández Retamar did, traditional concepts of civilization and barbarism.

Zea sees a further parallel in the blacks' affirmation of blackness or "Africanity" and the Latin Americans' affirmation of "Latinoamericanity." Blacks, he observes, affirm their blackness not to isolate themselves but to stand on their ethnic identity in the company of those cultures they assimilate. Paraphrasing Senghor, he writes that with the black it is a question of incorporating and of assimilating but not of being incorporated and assimilated. In other words, the black does not want to stop being black so as to be white. In like manner, Latin Americans do not want to stop being Latin American in order to be European or Anglo-Saxon. Here, too, it is a question of assimilating and incorporating, but without being assimilated and incorporated. In other words, Zea seems to argue, accept what Europe and the West have to offer but do not become dependent and, above all, do not stop being what one is. Europe and the West should take from the black, as from the Latin American, and become enriched with what different cultures have to offer.

Zea applies the term *depersonalization*—which Senghor and René Dépestre used in earlier discussions of black identity—to the plight of Latin Americans who assimilate foreign ways too eagerly, adding that this term also describes what José Enrique Rodó was trying to do in his *Ariel* (1900), where he combated *nordomanía,* or outright imitation of Anglo-Saxon culture from the United States. *Négritude, indigenismo,* and *latinoamericanismo,* then, should ideally take from others without giving up what is indigenous to these qualities as they define one's own past identity. To totally deny the ethnic component of one's past is just as bad as proclaiming, as Sarmiento did, "Civilization or barbarism!" Both attitudes inspired Fernández Retamar's call for a new reading of Latin American history, culture, and literature, one that explicitly rejected Sarmiento's views.

Fernández Retamar's *Calibán* does not renounce the past in favor of a "foreign" future. In like manner Zea also argued that renunciation of one's roots leaves one open to colonialism and to new forms of dependency he sees operant not only in Latin America but in Africa and in Asia as well. In this regard, Zea insists, *négritude* and *indigenismo* have something to teach, or to offer, namely, a spirit of independence that others can draw from in their own struggles for liberation and decolonialization. Fernández Retamar has written that in Fanon's book "we find not a few observations applicable to us Latin Americans. Although Fanon is addressing Africa, his broad outline applies to a common problem in all of our countries."[7] The Cuban author refers to the role of the *campesino*, guerrilla warfare, and new revolutionary organizations, but the most significant parallel, one could argue, relates to Ché Guevara's advice to "paint yourselves black." This advice best underscores the tie to Fanon, to Guillén's ethnocentric *son* and to the reversal of symbols Fernández Retamar effected with his theory of a Latin American literature that recognizes its cultural, racial, and historical roots.

When black literature dealing with the black experience is produced by those whose problems are under focus rather than by well-meaning but outside observers, literary expression becomes a genuine example of "authentic communication," unblocked by obstacles of race, class, and foreign vision that prevent "seeing and understanding the cultures of the exploited in Latin America."[8] Afro-Hispanic authors provide examples as genuine as the very strong Afro models presented by Franz Fanon and by such negritude authors as Aimé Césaire and Leon Damas with their "active look, a fighting look, a revolutionary look."[9] More even than the *indigenista* authors, who have erroneously been called Latin America's closest parallels to the French *négritude* writers,[10] such Spanish-American *négritude* writers as Nicolás Guillén, Nelson Estupiñán Bass, and Nicomedes Santa Cruz provide Latin America with homegrown models who have the same active look, fighting look, and revolutionary look—and indeed the same humanistic outlook—as their Afro-French counterparts. Afro-Hispanic authors are known for these same qualities.

Black contributions in general to new-world culture are not limited to song, dance, and emotion, though these qualities, too, are significant. Other factors that have to be considered include independence, revolt, and humanism. Also, the black writer's awareness of the cultural and national significance of his own literature has to be recognized. Nicolás Guillén not only rejects "foxtrot" culture but *negrista* poetry as well, which he considers more superficial and certainly less authentic than his own. Manuel Zapata Olivella writes a committed literature built on local needs and problems in Colombia and predicated on local solutions free from foreign models. His fellow Afro-Colombian Carlos Arturo Truque opposes unrestricted subjugation to foreign cultures. Juan Pablo Sojo in Venezuela rejects Rómulo Gallegos's *Pobre negro* as less authentic a depiction of the Barlovento region and its black inhabitants than *Nochebuena negra*, his own black novel. Adalberto Ortiz turns away from the white aesthetic in his Afro-Ecuadorian poetry and fiction. The list is long and goes back to the nineteenth century with Plácido's rejection of Spain and with Candelario Obeso's emphasis on the local forms of popular speech and poetry as the only true way to build an authentic and original Colombian literature worthy of the name. In his Afro-Colombian literature, as in Nicolás Guillén's Afro-Cuban literature, literary blackness and literary Americanism come together.

Black authors insist that their expressions of literary Americanism are authentic, which makes it difficult to classify their work, as Gordon Brotherston[11] does, as mere "vernacular" literature. More meaningful is Segrade's attempt to see black, Indian, and *gaucho* literary expressions as true representatives of "The American Voice." That this voice can be a black one is further supported by such authors as Candelario Obeso, Nicolás Guillén, Gaspar Octavio Hernández, and even by the eighteenth-century improviser El Negrito Poeta and the slave poet Juan Francisco Manzano, who see themselves not only as blacks but as thoroughly Hispanisized blacks writing a black language out of racial, nationalistic, and patriotic dedication. They believe, in short, that their language is the language of a people as representative of the larger society as any other.

Gordon Brotherston dismisses pre-Colombian Indian literature, arguing that literature of the American native belongs to the history not of Latin but of Indian American literature. This kind of argument cannot be used against black literature because it is being cultivated today. Further, black Hispanic writers do not show the paternalism and the ambivalence of the "select minority," some of whom had to disguise themselves before going out among the masses to learn their ways; nor do they have to heed Ché Guevara's symbolic suggestion "paint yourselves black" that has been ridiculed by Emir Rodríguez Mongeal.[12] When Jean Franco[13] speaks of the problems of the intellectual who finds himself in difficulty when dealing with the original culture of the people and their rich oral tradition, she is not talking about black writers, because they are part of that culture. No white elite could possibly regard itself as representative of the nation or the subcontinent, she has argued, but the same cannot be said of nonwhite intellectuals who wrote out of a familiarity, born of an ethnic and class kinship, that has enriched both their literary expression and the concept of literary Americanism.

Unlike *mundonovista* novelists who before incorporating ethnic reality into their novels had to journey "into back country to observe, record and protect,"[14] such black novelists as Juan Pablo Sojo and Arnoldo Palacios were not "doomed to failure" since what they wrote about was not "marginal to the novelists' own experience."[15] The "unbridgeable gap" that separated the novelists from their material that D. P. Gallagher writes about cannot be applied to black novelists. When he writes that regional novels are rarely authentic or convincing since they are about "them," not "us," he cannot be talking about the black regional novel in Latin America. He is correct, however, in asserting that the regional novel, despite its humanistic concern, "is all too often a patronizing attempt on the part of a usually urban author to present alien, exotic material to an urban market."[16]

Black Hispanic literature is deeply rooted in local conditions and needs and is an authentic expression of literary Americanism not only because it arises from within one of the significant ethnic components of Latin America but also because that literature, while written within the black literary tradition of protest, is at the same time representative of the concerns, styles, and literary movements associated with Latin America as a whole. Black literature in Latin America has its own parallel history, but one that should not detract from the enrichment the African legacy brings to the larger body of Latin American literature. Gaspar Octavio Hernández carried the nickname "The Black Swan," but he was also known as Panama's foremost modernist poet. Arnoldo Palacios's *Las estrellas son negras* is a very "black" book, but it is as well perhaps Colombia's outstanding naturalist novel. Plácido was shot partly because of his color, which made it easier for the authorities to read seditious and racial sentiment into his poetry. But Plácido was Cuba's romantic poet whose *criollo* verse was partly responsible for founding a distinctively Cuban, as opposed to the Castillian, school of poetry. Adalberto Ortiz's *Juyungo*, Juan Pablo Sojo's *Nochebuena negra*, and Manuel Zapata Olivella's *Corral de negros* are "black" novels, but they are as well Latin American novels of the *selva* (jungle), of the land, and of the city, respectively. The parallel continues in the new novels of Carlos Guillermo Wilson ("Cubena"), Quince Duncan, and Nelson Estupiñán Bass, and in Manuel Zapata Olivella's newest novel, *Changó, el gran putas* (1983), which is as much about America as it is about American roots in Africa.

Afro-Hispanic models have their own literary history, but one that becomes paradigmatic of the whole of Latin America, especially when authentic responses to dependency are sought. Magic realism understood ethnocentrically is a way out of dependence, and the role model black literature provides as an authentic alternative must be emphasized. But the most promising black contribution lies in oral literature or ethnopoetics, which forces recognition of oral cultures that have for centuries escaped dependency status. Such black authors as Candelario Obeso, Carlos Arturo Truque, Nicolás Guillén, Nelson Estupiñán Bass, and Abdias do Nascimento in Brazil insist, as Leopoldo Lugones and others have done, that a national literature has to be built from the ground up, that is, from popular sources of folk untouched by foreign influences.

Echoing Fernández Retamar's criticism of Sarmiento, Jean Franco has written that in early Latin America "progress was so closely associated with print that Sarmiento, for instance, could dismiss oral history and literature as curiosities which it was irrelevant to collect."[17] That attitude was unfortunate, for as she explains, due must be given to the oral within the context of a dependent culture because only at that level of discourse was the colonized culture able to keep alive "the dynamic and subversive aspects of popular tradition."[18] Franco singles out within this context the oral improvisations of El Negrito Poeta, the eighteenth-century black poet in Mexico whose "witty responses delivered in perfect *coplas* helped him to mock at the erudite and protect himself from racial slights."[19] José Hernández attempted to capture the same kind of wit and mocking vitality of the folk voice, Franco argues, in his *Martín Fierro*. She also believes even Pablo Neruda used the sense of immediacy and communal participation of oral performance in his *Canto general*. J. B. Kubayanda[20] recently insisted further on the significance of African orality in Afro-Hispanic texts.

A Modern Black Everyman

The communal participation of oral performance also can be found in the improvisations of Nelson Estupiñán Bass's black singers Timarán and Cuabú, two excellent examples of the didactic potential of oral literature from the popular tradition. Nowhere in recent black Latin American literature is the black better presented as defender of the homeland and guardian of national culture than in the *poesía popular* (and in the novel) of Nelson Estupiñán Bass. The recent fiction of this Afro-Ecuadorian writer, is rooted in the black voices he created first in *Timarán y Cuabú*[21] (1956) and, more recently, in *El desempate* (1978).[22] Timarán and Cuabú are two outspoken Afro-Hispanic *payadores* (singers) in the *gaucho* tradition who are strongly reminiscent of Guillén's own powerful black voices (José Ramón Cantaliso, Juan el Barbero). *El desempate* is a continuation and culmination of the long verbal battle these two singers began in *Timarán y Cuabú*, and the match-up in this second volume represents modern social lyricism at its best because it serves, as the earlier volume had done, to teach racial, social, cultural, national, political, and humanistic consciousness through the use of popular folk forms transposed into written literature.

Popular poetry is extremely important in Estupiñán Bass's didactic view of art because popular poetry teaches. The author's latest novels attack "vende-patrias" and corrupt officials who sell out to foreign powers, and they focus on the sovereignty of Ecuadorian oil. But even in 1956, Estupiñán Bass in *contrapunteo* form was defending his country against the humiliation of the "foreign yoke";[23] he continues to be just as protective now, even defending Ecuadorian culture against the culture of "el rocanrol,"[24] a term that carries the same negative symbolism for him in the 1980s as did "foxtrot" culture for Guillén in the 1930s.

The *contrapunteo* is a poetic mechanism for airing contrasting views, or for presenting both sides of important issues, but on a popular level. Estupiñan Bass's verbal battles are not philosophical riddles but timely arguments that raise significant human questions in a Third World context. Nationalization of natural resources and agrarian reform are two of these issues, but beyond these concerns his popular poetry debates the pros and cons of such topics as women's liberation, birth control, the new morality, and hypocrisy in government.

The *contrapunteo* in *Timarán y Cuabú* ends in a tie, but in the second volume Cuabú emerges the clear winner largely because of the firmness of his response on the question of race. There are many themes in *El desempate*, but the key verses, I believe, insofar as the new American voice is concerned, focus on the racial composition of the two singers, and on their understanding of their racial significance. The mulatto Timarán believes himself to be "la mejor materia prima / de la América nueva" (the best raw material / of the new America) and chooses to side with his "hermano negro" (black brother) and his "hermano indio" (Indian brother),[25] but it is Alberto Cuabú, the black, who emerges the overall winner. Cuabú wins partly because he puts himself forward literally as a modern black everyman:

Soy de aquí y todas partes	I am from here and everywhere
yo marcho de tumbo en tumbo	and I go from sea to sea
y he renunciado mi patria	and I have renounced my country
porque mi patria es el mundo.	because my country is the world.

Soy como el judío errante,	I am like the Wandering Jew,
no me importan las banderas,	national boundaries do not matter to
pues para los hombres pobres	me
no se han hecho las fronteras.²⁶	since poor people
	spill over everywhere

Cuabú clarifies his role in *El desempate* as his everyman theme embraces specific marginal groups in the Third World:

Ahora soy	Now I am
el amenazante Poder Negro en Norte	the threatening fist of Black Power in
América	North America
el horno socialista en Africa	the socialist hotbed in Africa
el moreno que forja	the mulatto forging a new dawn in
un alba nueva en el Brasil	Brazil
el embrión del viento nuevo en las	the new wind beginning to blow in
Antillas	the Antilles
bomba de tiempo en Panama,	a time bomb in Panama,
el ébano alegre en Ecuador	joyful black ebony in Ecuador
el zambo	the Zambo
el moreno	the man of color
el marginado sutilmente aquí y allá.²⁷	subtly kept on the outside
	everywhere

Cuabú the black gets the deciding vote and wins because he speaks unashamedly and unreservedly as a black voice of America. In casting his tie-breaking vote for Cuabú, the judge characterizes him as a

Nuevo Mandinga gigante	A great new Mandingo voice
pregón de la *multitú*	who crying out for the masses
que dará a la *negritú*	will give to blackness
la *juerza* del huracán.²⁸	a hurricane strength.

In *El desempate* Alberto Cuabú's "Mandingo voice" becomes, like Juyungo's, a new American voice. The *negritú* of this "Nuevo Mandinga gigante" becomes the spokesman for the *multitú,* and the author hopes that the youth of the country in the future will unite with this multitude.

Estupiñán Bass leaves little doubt that this new "voz de esperanza" (voice of hope) is a black one. By making Cuabú the new American voice, Nelson Estupiñán Bass, as Nicolás Guillén and Adalberto Ortiz had done early in this century, gives a major role to the black in his quest for an authentic Latin American identity.

Black Humanism

Nelson Estupiñán Bass's black spokesmen again turn our attention to the communal stance, the cornerstone of literary Americanism and of *la especifidad latinoamericana*. When this stance grows out of the "unofficial activities and responses of the people,"[29] we understand why oral performance "helps us to detect the weaknesses of certain critics (including structuralists) whose exclusive concern with print needs correction."[30] Black oral performance is no exception. The black experience in the New World is paradigmatic of literary Americanism in Latin America and, it has been argued, of the non-Western experience of all native peoples as well. What is more, black literature offers Western culture itself a new humanism in the form of a set of humanist values that draws heavily on oral literature, which to many has become the key to any valid responses to dependency.

The humanist values of the black experience, which are reflected in Afro-Hispanic literature, help make it easier to understand the significance of that literature as a representative model for literary Americanism. This conclusion is unavoidable when we accept that humanism and a communal stance are key elements not only of the concept of literary Americanism but of Afro-Hispanic literature as well. Perhaps nowhere are humanistic questions more specifically applicable or relevant than to black literature, including that written in Latin America. For the *mundonovista* novelists, as for the true giants of Latin American poetry, humanism and literary Americanism were one and the same thing. For the black writer in Latin America, humanism, literary Americanism, and literary blackness are one and the same thing as well, since the black writer assumes the same communal stance as the larger Latin American literature.

Afro-Hispanic writers, then, are authentic representatives of literary Americanism not only because they write from within but also because they rarely betray the Latin American tradition of social protest. Black writers in Latin America and elsewhere for the most part have confronted what Addison Gayle, Jr., has called the "age-old" dichotomy between literature as artifact and literature as a vehicle for the liberation of a people.[31] This is not to say that black writers do not combine humanistic and social concerns with art, only that they want their literature to "mean" more than simply "be." Perhaps more importantly, in Latin America black writers like Nicolás Guillén have not "played" to the mainstream audience other than by "digging down" in search of the universal in the particular.

The principle of nonneutrality in art governs the kind of advocacy stance many Afro-Hispanic authors take. This stance seems essential to any author who suspects that too much emphasis on form, aesthetics, and art for art's sake could, in fact, be a cover for more serious failures, such as "an aggressive camouflage for racism, or a willful defense of caste and priviledge."[32] In black literature in Latin America, moral persuasion, subjective identification, and such themes as freedom, liberty, and justice reflect social and humanistic concerns. Like all great literature much black literature in Latin America is written "to protest some aspect of the human condition."[33]

Human solidarity is evident in Afro-Hispanic literature, where man's inhumanity to man is just as much a thematic constant as in Latin American literature as a whole. This does not mean, however, that there is a shift from black concerns, only that there is room in black literature for more. Black writers like Nicolás Guillén, Manuel Zapata Olivella, Nelson Estupiñán Bass, and Nicomedes Santa Cruz move outward from the black experience and what it tells us about man's inhumanity to man to a larger concern for anyone down and out. Again, there is the move from the specific to the general, from black protest to a humanism that speaks "to the inhumanity of his times,"[34] particularly when that inhumanity is based on differences that regard some races or classes as inferior.

The new humanism in Latin America, by building on ethnocentric recognition of the *mestizo*, the mulatto, the Indian, and the black, incorporates part of what in Senghor's estimation makes up two-thirds of humanity. What he described as "the call of man to man," or interest in the elementary needs of justice, brotherhood, and love, has long been a thematic constant of negritude which Senghor's book *Negritude and Humanism*[35] indicates. These needs are not just abstractions in black literature. Black humanism, it has been argued, moves beyond abstractions and focuses on human individuals and their experiences, which explains Albert Gérard's theory that there is an "emotional personalism"[36] in black humanism, and his insistence that there are differences between black humanism and white humanism.[37]

Richard Wright has argued that humanistic communism is too abstract and not sufficiently based on human feelings and lived experience. Gérard augments this theory by insisting that all "white" humanism is too abstract and anonymous, arguing that "black" humanism is more personally identified with the suffering of particular individuals. Gérard's position, in short, is that in "black" humanism, there is less of the "abstraction of the party line" or the "anonymity of general theories." What both Wright and Gérard push for, in effect, is an essential humanism that rises above not only the rigidity of formalism but the abstraction and rigidity of ideology as well. Rather than allow humanism to remain in the abstract, black writers in Latin America, such as Ortiz in *Juyungo*, use individual black experiences as points of departure in developing such themes as revolt, justice, and freedom. Black writers in Latin America insist, through an essential subjectivism, on giving their humanism, socialist or otherwise, a black touch. This *toque negro* makes the literature of such black authors as Nicolás Guillén stand out as black even when recognized for its Third World, proletarian, or universal expression.

Humanism, then, like the assertion of blackness, is a common organizing principle among negritude writers in general.[38] In Latin America Adalberto Ortiz, for example, classified himself as a humanist writer in a recent interview with Gunter Lorenz.[39] J. Gallegos Lara backs this up by comparing Ortiz's humanistic outlook in *Juyungo* to Richard Wright's.[40] Carl Pederson recognizes Manuel Zapata Olivella's "great humanistic power"[41] in the Afro-Colombian author's novel *Corral de negros,* which is, in the first instance, a demand for justice for blacks. Carlos Guillermo Wilson, through strong humanistic protest on behalf of blacks, expresses his love for humanity in his Afro-Panamanian poetry and prose. Victorio Llanos Allende and Pilar Barrios represent black humanistic values in Puerto Rico and Uruguay, respectively. Quince Duncan writes a Costa Rican prose that is very concerned with the humanity of his black and nonblack protagonists. Even Regino Pedroso's famous poem "Hermano negro" points as much to what is universally human in his subject as to what is specifically black. Humanism continues to be important in the works of Nelson Estupiñán Bass, a profoundly humane and humanistic writer.

The body of Afro-humanistic literature is large, and is available from older writers still evolving and from younger ones just beginning. All see themselves as black authors writing in the tradition of literary Americanism, even when that tradition is seen in the context of a "new stage" exemplified by the Cuban Revolution. René Dépestre[42] has made a case against "mystical" ties with Africa as compared to total identification with the new nation of the new-world black. He considers Nicolás Guillén a classic example of the national taking precedence over a universal black aesthetic. Guillén himself explained to Keith Ellis in a recent interview that the struggle in Cuba had to be a revolutionary struggle to abolish the division of society into classes since this division, Guillén argued, was the source of racism in Cuba.[43] Guillén continues to write about abuses blacks suffer throughout the world, but he has adapted his poetry to the national needs of his country which, following the revolution, is "cohesive reconstruction."[44] Guillén's ability to adapt, Ellis contends, and to define and elaborate artistically at different times in his nation's history its legitimate concerns has made him Cuba's national poet by popular acclaim. This same ability makes his work not only "perfectly adapted" to the needs of postrevolutionary society in Cuba but also representative of that "new stage" of literary Americanism.

This new stage of patriotic identification links blacks who have remained in Cuba as much with national liberation as with black liberation, though as Lorna Williams has pointed out,[45] Guillén believes that
blacks are the primary beneficiaries of the revolution in that country.
The communal stance that Guillén assumes in his poetry speaks of the
"possibility of harmonious relations in an ideal community, in which all
obvious social differences are erased."[46] This "blurring" of the bound-
aries between the self and the other has been examined by Williams in
Self and Society, one of the most recent accounts of the socialist consciousness that Guillén blends in with his black consciousness. This
compatible mixture lies at the core of the humanistic vision he imposes
on his concept of literary Americanism, a vision that, though rooted in
the African legacy, moves his work beyond black, social, and revolutionary concerns to a larger concern with the fate of man and society in
general. Guillén's belief in the perfectability of man and society, Williams argues, is his most recent contribution to the social poetry that has
long characterized literary Americanism in Latin America.

A basic theme in Guillén's poetry is human beings, not just black people
or working-class people or socialists. This all-encompassing concern
makes Guillén's poetry of more than just ideological or racial interest. It
also, his supporters would argue, makes his search for a humanistic
formula for literary Americanism adaptable not only to Cuba but to other
Latin American countries as well—wherever human freedoms are limited. Guillén's essential humanism links his Cuban version of negritude as
Dépestre understands it to socialist government in that country and to the
wider collective experience that Pablo Neruda and César Vallejo sought in
their humanistic poetry. What Guillén has in common with these other
giants of twentieth-century Latin American poetry is that his work, like
theirs, is very deeply rooted in a specific ethnic new-world figure, which
moves his poetry, like theirs, beyond an abstract ideological stage. As
Coulthard put it: "The essentialist poetry of Nicolás Guillén is a signal
of man discovering himself completely in his concrete American reality,
and at the same time transferring through his individuality the ethical
pathos of his people. Like any Afro-American and Indo-American writer,

Guillén has found his national, American and universal identity, his Cuban, American and profoundly humanist values."[47]

That Guillén is a "humanist and ambassador plenipotentiary of Cuba"[48] does not detract from his reputation of being one of the Caribbean's most accomplished innovators in poetry, a reputation built, in the first instance, on his bold insistence on incorporating stylistic peculiarities from the black oral tradition in Cuba to formal print literature and, ultimately, to the flexibility this incorporation allows him in his poetic handling of traditional Spanish verse forms. Guillén's reputation for seeing black anguish and specific Cuban problems as part of the wider struggle of humanity for justice and equality is indeed enhanced by his "way with words" and by the way literary blackness defines his poetry whether seen as black poetry, as authentic expressions of *criollo* poetry or of *la cubanidad*, or simply as literary Americanism. Guillén's own advice is not to just write social poetry but to write a "beautiful social poetry,"[49] and his counsel to young poets is "romper el soneto" (break up the sonnet) not "romper *con* el soneto" (break *with* the sonnet). "But do it with the artistry this demanding form requires, and fill that form with a burning social commitment and revolutionary force as you seek fulfillment that ideologically is both human and forward looking."[50]

Guillén continues to follow his own advice in his later works where he combined artistic concern with social preoccupations. His *El diario que a diario* (1972) has, in fact, been described as "an artistically daring mixture of genres of poetry, of political caricature, journalism, advertisement writing, etc., to form a panorama of Cuba's historic evolution from colonial times to the Revolution of 1959."[51] Small wonder, therefore, that Guillén's broad range of metrical forms led José Antonio Portuondo to consider him a model for poets and artists in revolutionary Cuba.[52] Guillén's commitment to art and to essential humanism is shared by other black writers in Latin America who want to innovate, experiment, and "liven up" dead literature without losing touch or passing into the mainstream and oblivion. It is hardly coincidental, for example, that Nicolás Guillén and Nelson Estupiñán Bass, both authors of "beautiful" social literature, are as known for their anti-academic "poetry of the people" as for their mastery of the erudite and set forms of literature. Break up the sonnet, not break with it, Guillén has said. In like manner Estupiñán Bass, as we shall see, breaks up the novel form without breaking with it.

Nicolás Guillén, Nelson Estupiñán Bass, Nicomedes Santa Cruz, and others all exemplify the ethnic nature of literary Americanism. By placing their literature squarely on the side of the proletariat they, like Langston Hughes (if we judge by his "Daybreak in Alabama," the last poem in *The Panther and the Lash*, his last book of poems), envision a union of black and white. Nicolás Guillén, certainly in his celebrated "La muralla" ("The Wall") wants to use "white hands and black hands" to complete this vision. Once having revealed black people in the "full strength of their humanity"[53] Nicolás Guillén and his Afro-Hispanic colleagues turned their communal voices to the humanity of others, thus raising their concern to a broader humanistic level shared by all Latin American authors who have at heart the same desire for liberty, justice, and freedom.

The closest counterpart to Nicolás Guillén in Brazil, perhaps, is Solano Trindade (1908–1974), whose poetry, especially in *Contares au meu povo*, (1961), identifies with all oppressed people whether black or white. Trindade's poetry is "black based"[54] (written by a black on behalf of blacks) but is nevertheless, and above all, against the inhumanity of all oppression. Like Guillén, Trindade identifies with his African heritage, but sees himself and his fellow Afro-Brazilians as inextricably linked to America and its future. Equally significant, Trindade, like Guillén, was an exponent of a universal humanism with which he saw the black establishing solidarity.[55] Trindade's black consciousness and his message of universal brotherhood are continued in the recent poetry of Eduardo de Oliveira. Oliveira's humanism, however, was inspired not by revolution, as was the case with Trindade, but by a type of love which will respect the status quo. Oliveira, especially in his last collection of poems, *Gestas liricas da negritude* (1967), sees negritude as the black man's contribution to the humanization of the white man's world.[56]

Black writers in Latin America have done much to raise the social, political, and racial consciousness of their readers. Like Nicolás Guillén, whose whole life has reflected a search for an authentic Cuban and ultimately an authentic Latin American identity, they have battled and continue to battle against an exclusively white, Eurocentric approach to Cuban and Latin American culture. Guillén's own running battle ranges from his *son* poems in the 1930s to more recent poems like "Paris" and "Problemas del subdesarrollo" and especially "Qué color?" where he defends Martin Luther King's right to a black soul, one "black as coal." Such quests for authenticity typify the widespread desire of Cubans and of Latin Americans in general to redirect their own political, cultural, and economic orientation. This ethnocentric redirection can be called "reversing symbols," as I prefer, or it can be seen as part of ongoing attempts "to alter the existing asymmetrical arrangements in Spanish America's favor."[57] Whatever the terminology, the black model in Latin America has a role to play in the search for the true American voice.

Chapter Five

The Continuing Quest

It has been the fate of the Afro-American writer to be preoccupied with setting history straight.

—John M. Reilly

Coming Full Circle

New black authors in Latin America continue a humanistic quest not unlike the new response furthered by Roberto Fernández Retamar's *Calibán* (1971), a work whose significance, in part, lies in the rejection of the belief that white is always good and nonwhite bad, savage, and barbaric. This belief is also rejected in Latin America by black writers whose literature clearly forms part of a humanizing process that sees civilization and barbarism come full circle. As part of this process new black novelists in Latin America move beyond the black literary tradition and bring ethnic balance to the larger Latin American sensibility while injecting it with persistent calls for a cultural and political independence and for sanity in race relations as well.

In their continuing quest for balance black Hispanic novelists today are producing works in prose comparable in achievement and humanistic intent to Nicolás Guillén's poetry. Recent black fiction in Spanish began to appear in the early 1960s in Colombia with Manuel Zapata Olivella's *Corral de negros* (1963) and other novels by him acclaimed for their artistry and continued to evolve in the late 1960s with Adalberto Ortiz's *El espejo y la ventana* (1967). The evolution accelerated in the 1970s with the appearance of several experimental novels by Ortiz's fellow Ecuadorian Nelson Estupiñán Bass, Jorge Artel's first novel—*No es la muerte, es el morir* (1979)—in Colombia, and the first publications of Quince Duncan in Costa Rica. The black novel entered a new phase in the 1980s in Panama with Carlos Guillermo Wilson's *Chombo* (1981) and his yet unpublished *Afroexiliados,* the first two volumes of a projected trilogy. *Sodinú,* the third and final volume, is under way. The acknowledged masters of the black novel in Spanish also continue to produce in the 1980s: Estupiñán Bass's most recent novel, *Bajo el cielo nublado,* appeared in mid-1981, and he has completed *El crepúsculo,* his most recent novel. Manuel Zapata Olivella's *Changó, el gran putas,* fifteen years in preparation, appeared in 1983, as did Adalberto Ortiz's *La envoltura del sueño* and Juan Zapata Olivella's *Historia de un joven negro* (1983). Juan Zapata Olivella also published his second novel, *Pisando el camino de ébano,* a year later.

While Zapata Olivella's *Changó, el gran putas* is the newest and most ambitious of the new black fiction in Spanish (see chapter 6), the recent novels of Quince Duncan, Carlos Guillermo Wilson, Nelson Estupiñán Bass, Jorge Artel, and Juan Zapata Olivella stand as important landmarks in the humanizing tendencies of black Hispanic literature. Duncan and Wilson, or "Cubena" as he prefers to be called, provide us with insights into the little-known black literature of Central America, while Nelson Estupiñán Bass in Ecuador shows black and Third World concerns expressed through a multiplicity of novelistic techniques. These six authors speak out for human rights and represent very well the humanistic quest that characterizes black literature and black life throughout the Americas.

To begin with, the link between black Hispanic literature and the humanizing process that brought civilization and barbarism full circle in Latin America is nowhere better illustrated than in Quince Duncan's *La paz del pueblo* (1978). In Duncan's novel the followers of Marcus Garvey in Costa Rica represent to some observers a "barbarism" associated with Africa. The term, however, is used in a different sense in the novel because it connotes change for the better through collective strike action that will deliberately upset the somnambulant patterns of a town peaceful on the surface. Duncan's first novel, *Los cuatro espejos* (1973), moved from the interior search for identity of his black protagonist, who had internalized the social and racial problems that characterize Costa Rican society, outward toward wider humanistic relationships. *La paz del pueblo* continues in this same broad vein.

In the true tradition of literary Americanism Duncan's recent novel addresses issues of justice, human dignity, and the liberation of a people, and he builds his message through complex structures and religious symbolisms both biblical (European) and Afro-folk (African). The syncretic nature of his message is reflected in the characterization of Pedro Dull, the protagonist. Pedro is "on the one hand the epitomy of the spirit of radical liberation in the Judeo-Christian tradition, being a Messiah figure. On the other hand, as an embodiment of *cumina,* he is a forceful representative of the Afro American revolutionary religious tradition, a tradition that has engendered such phenomena as the voodoo-inspired Haitian Revolution, the Aponte rebellion in Cuba, the Morant Bay rebellion in Jamaica, and the contemporary Black Power Movement in the United States."[1]

Though couched in the syncretism of new-world religion, *La paz del pueblo* is a novel of black rebellion. Structurally ambitious like some of Nelson Estupiñán Bass's recent work, and symbolic like Cubena's use of ancestral myths (and new ones of his own creation), Duncan's novel seeks "salvation" (better working conditions) through the revolutionary efforts of the "barbaric" followers of Marcus Garvey, not through faith in a white civilization that oppresses black people. Duncan's quest for balance is a syncretic quest, but while syncretism is "an essential creative force in his art,"[2] his ultimate goal is the same reversal of symbols brought to fruition in the new phase of literary Americanism that Carlos Guillermo Wilson's works represent.

Reversing Symbols

Wilson's novels are, in part, autobiographical statements, but they are also much more than his own personal history. Continuing where he left off with his *Pensamientos del negro Cubena* (1977) and *Cuentos del negro Cubena* (1977), Wilson also turns to Marcus Garvey, using a quote from this black leader on the title page of *Chombo* (1981): "A people without knowledge of their past history, origin and culture is like a tree without roots." This quote generally sets the tone for all of Cubena's work and reflects specifically the organizing principle on which the structure of *Chombo*, through flashback form, is built. This principle, quite simply, is a people's quest for freedom and for respect of human rights. *Chombo*, like *Afroexiliados*, is a strong statement that not only calls on blacks to remember their history but also cautions whites not to overlook the black contribution in the history, origin, and culture of the Panamanian nation.

Chombo could be subtitled "A Week in the Life of Lito," an angry young black recently returned from abroad at the time of the Carter-Torrijos treaty negotiations. Lito's concern with the negotiations' effects on blacks in Panama form the contemporary backdrop against which *Chombo* is set, even though the novel is interwoven with the black history of Panama, the West Indies, and Africa. The narration, through flashback, the recounting of legends and tales, and the discussion of current events, traces the ordeals and experiences of one family of "Afro exiles," as Cubena calls blacks in the New World. Historical perspective is important in both novels as the author carefully frames the personal story he is telling with references to political and historical events in this century and before. Regarding the 1950s, for example, a proposed trip back to Jamaica in *Chombo* becomes, for Lito's family, the most important event of a decade in which the following took place:

General McArthur was fired . . . Puerto Rico achieved associated statehood . . . the nationalism of Jomo Kenyatta in Kenya . . . the death of Stalin . . . the return of the Shah of Iran . . . segregation declared unconstitutional in the United States . . . Perón overthrown in Argentina . . . The nationalization of the Suez Canal. Somoza assassinated in Nicaragua . . . Russia put Sputnik I in orbit . . . The independence of Ghana . . . the death of Pope Pius XII . . . Castro's revolution . . .[3]

Historical reference is important, but the inside view of the *chombo*, or the West Indian in Panama, gives the novel its power. The story of such memorable individuals as James Duglin, or Papá James, and Nenén rewrites history to include a black point of view, as does Cubena's tribute to his African ancestors who came over in the "second crossing" seven decades ago from the Antilles to Panama to work on the canal, "The Big Ditch." *Chombo* is an attempt to reclaim black dignity and recognition, and the author does this by recounting his own experiences and those of other descendants and their African ancestors. In neither of the two novels does Cubena overlook any of the hardships the *chombo* encountered in Panama, from the system of segregation and discrimination called Gold Roll and Silver Roll (which paid whites double in gold and blacks at a lower rate in silver for the same work) to the many hazards that caused deaths among blacks, such as malaria, yellow fever, pneumonia, derailments, explosions, and landslides. In addition, blacks had to suffer racist insults and the dehumanizing effect of the white aesthetic.

The hatred, prejudice, and disrespect shown toward *chombos* in Panama are inspired not only by their color but by their Protestant religion, their foreign origin, and their use of English as a first language. Cubena is devasting also in his criticism of Hispanic blacks who for some of these same reasons show resentment of the Panamanian black of West Indian origin. Included in his criticism is Cubena's rejection of *mestizaje* or *blanqueamiento,* as he believes this desire for whiteness characterizes the Hispanic or the "Colonial Black" who, like Karafula Barrescoba, proudly declared

that she was a colonial Black like those who founded Old Panama, and not an inferior West Indian Black like Nenén . . . Karafula Barrescoba felt superior to the West Indians because her mother tongue was Spanish, her religion Catholic and especially because race mixture has bleached out some of her blackness. She emphasized every chance she got that she was not black, mulatto, yes, but not black. She got very upset if someone took her for a West Indian. Each time she saw a person of West Indian descent she let out a shout and immediately powdered her face. She would go to the "La Chola" beauty salon to have her hair straightened. And every night before going to bed she would pinch her nose shut with a hair pin so that it would be less flat in the morning, and when she got up in the morning she would go through her skin whitening routine, soaking herself in five cans of white milk. (P. 65)

In another "history" lesson standard history books overlook, Cubena argues against this division, this time in a classroom lecture:

Luisa, the black teacher, always started her lecture declaring how absurd it is to divide the Panamanian Blacks in two groups: Colonial Blacks and West Indian Blacks because creoles or the Blacks of West Indian ancestry are actually more colonial than the so-called colonial Blacks since the latter were no longer considered colonials after the beginning of the nineteenth century when Panama was no longer a Spanish colony. West Indian Blacks, on the other hand, were "colonials" until Jamaica obtained independence in '62 and Barbados in '66 . . . Furthermore, she added, all Blacks have the same black mother—Africa. (P. 88)

Other "lessons" in black history refer to black workers and injustices they endured over the years. Cubena also reminds us that Panama had its share of heroic freedom fighters as well. In addition to the Marcus Garveys and the Cudjoes and the countless numbers who gave their lives in the construction of the Canal there are other memorable figures in the history of the *chombo* in Panama, such as William Preston Stoute, "a black teacher born in Barbados," who "led protests against injustice" (p. 89) and was stripped of his Panamanian citizenship and deported to Cuba. Cubena, whose novels are gold mines of important but little-known facts of the black experience in Latin America, the Caribbean, and especially Panama, also credits blacks among the early anti-imperialists by recounting the many attempts by black revolutionary leaders who, "allergic to injustice," tried, for example, to liberate the city of Colón "from the Yankee yoke."

The strength of *Chombo* lies in Cubena's well-defined characters. Lito, for example, is a black protagonist for our times. A well-read young man, he has read *Roots* (in the original), and he constantly has the issues of today and yesterday on his mind. Lito laments the lost art of conversation, which has given way to television, because he is overflowing with information he wants to share about black Panamanian scholars, the First Congress of Black Culture in the Americas held in Cali, Colombia, in 1978, and childhood memories of the black presence in Panama. *Chombo*, like *Afroexiliados*, is a Panamanian *Roots* based in part on memories of conversations overheard in childhood by Lito, who blends these memories in with things he himself has seen. Lito is an angry but compassionate young black who has been around and has seen similarities in discrimination in the United States, South Africa, and Panama. His fury at times causes him to dream rebellion and wish revenge, a blood-letting "Judgment Day" when, fed up with injustice, he would with his own hand crush "white cockroaches, white rats, white dogs" (p. 96).

Cubena contrasts white characters in the novel with Lito, Papá James, Nenén, and other positive black figures. His depictions of whites are strongly negative and devasting ("white cockroaches, white rats, white dogs"), creating, some would say, amoral caricatures who harbor patho-logical hatred against blacks: the "poor devil" who wanted to become president of this country so that he would have the authority to deport all *chombos;* the fanatic official who believed "bleaching out Blacks is the way to build a country"; a Nazi sympathizer who is a member of a degenerate family; "the blind man with the white cane," whose blind-ness, perhaps, is symbolic of his unwillingness to see the black contribu-tion to Panama and who, while insisting on his own parentage with the Cid, the Catholic monarchs, and pure Spanish stock, affirms in a classic case of the prejudice of having no prejudice that there is no racial dis-crimination in Panama. Airport officials cannot tell English from French and, naturally, one black from another, and there is the "awful white woman next door" who hates all blacks, especially black women from the Antilles. Whites are generally abusive, ridiculous figures in *Chombo* and few escape Cubena's devastating depictions, whether they are doc-tors, school teachers, immigration officials, or simply racist neighbors, lesbians, or prostitutes. All are contrasted with the "great affection" blacks like Lito genuinely felt for their own.

Cubena is harsh in his negative characterizations of white antagonists, and in his retelling of the slave traffic—the "first crossing"—from Africa to the New World:

Never had this mass of black humanity seen such white horror. After satisfying their wanton appetites like disgusting hyenas these men of colorless white skin jampacked the slave ship with Blacks in chains . . . On the high seas the creaky ship rocked back and forth in time with the incessant cries from the bloody mass of blackness chained below. In the dark, stinking and flooded hold of the slave ship an army of white rats swam around with olympic skill in the abundant mixture of blood and excrement. The white rats satisfied their voracious appetites chewing out tongues and eyes and scurrying about in search of livers or other vital organs of the bodies of the dead Blacks. A frightened black girl in section five chained between two husky corpses . . . kept track of the time it took for this nauseating voyage to run its course: five menstruation periods it lasted. The young black women kept on deck were repeatedly raped . . . They were witnesses to the frequent orders of the Captain to throw many of the chained Blacks overboard into waters infested with white hungry sharks whenever there was danger of capsizing in hurricane winds. (Pp. 17–18)

Cubena is an effective storyteller, and much of the novel's originality derives from the author's refreshing willingness to unreservedly imbue his novel with a black perspective, one much influenced by the oral tales he passes on that were first related to him by his old *grani* ("abuelita"). In his account of the slave crossing, for example, Cubena reverses symbols (everything negative is white, not black), as he does throughout his novel, and he counts time much in the manner of an old storyteller. The transatlantic crossing took *cinco crepúsculos*, or *cinco menstruaciones*.

Cubena is an acute observer not just of the art of the oral tale but of today's changing manners and customs. He notes, for example, discourtesy among young people, and I have already mentioned his lament over the lost art of conversation. Cubena strikes a universal note in some of his observations, such as his regret that original homemade toys have been replaced with store-bought war games and television. But while his observations can be applied to changing customs and manners anywhere, there is no mistaking the Panamanian locale for his novel, as the author fills his pages with local nature, weather, street scenes, language, sights, sounds, and tastes. A very erudite author, Cubena resorts to the use of foreign languages and to classical and African mythological allusions, but he is equally at home with popular sententious sayings and with the language of the streets. The academic nature of his novel is rounded out with a glossary of Panamanian and Afro-Panamanian words, and he uses African words for the days of the week that serve as chapter titles. In a further display of his erudition Cubena uses quotations from seven different Afro-Spanish-American authors to head up those chapters.

Cubena has a fine sense of humor but one laced with biting irony and sarcasm. We see this humor in his choice of names—Mierdsié Leblancú, Carbón Barrescoba, Bartolomé Ladrón (alias Bartolomé Matanegros)—and in his defense of African names—such as Cubena, the one he himself carries—for new-world blacks. The argument in Panama against this practice of taking on African names is weak and humorous: "The teacher severely criticized his name for being so African, and asked him why West Indian Blacks did not adopt Panamanian names like Chiari, Wong, Heurtematte, Ghandi, Tagaropoulos" (p. 59). This teacher was taken to task by a black student who retorted:

The Chinese come here to this country and calmly give such names to their offspring as WONGCHANGCHOPSUIYE, and the Italians baptize theirs NEROGIUSEPPIESPAGUETTI, and nobody criticized this; but if the West Indian tries to preserve his African ties he is laughed at and even accused of being unpatriotic without taking into consideration that it was the West Indian Black who sweated and bled the most to build the railroad and the canal. (p. 59)

Cubena excels in descriptive passages that illustrate *tremendismo negrista*, which generally involves the description of abnormal, pathological, and racist behavior toward blacks or repulsive conditions bred of poverty, such as those in the Marañón district:

This was the most needy, the most scandalous, the most infested, the most rundown and the most licentious district of Panama. And to a certain extent this district was the last refuge of thieves, perverts, prostitutes, criminals . . .

In Marañón, a district devoid of trees and flowers but saturated with the smell of prostitutes and the vomit of drunks, the local children didn't play children's games . . . rather, they spent their time in these streets that stink of urine, spit, vomit, dog excrement and cheap whore perfume carrying on in vulgar street talk. (p. 76)

Much of this kind of description, however, is linked to the depraved behavior of whites, targets of the reversal of symbols prevalent throughout the novel. The slave passage was a *white horror*. The rats that devoured black bodies were *white rats*. The sharks that ate black bodies were *white* sharks. All of the negative forces in this novel are white. The color literally is a source of irritation even for a baby whose white diapers caused him diarrhea, whose white milk made him vomit, and who urinated on white uniforms and rejected white sugar, salt, flour, and cotton. The most *asquerosa* (disgusting) cockroaches in the novel are the *white* ones.

Cubena tries to balance things in *Chombo*. Too long, he seems to suggest, the color black has stood for negative, bad, and the opposite of virtue. He does a balancing act by raising the color black while demoting white. This is constantly true regardless of the story he is telling, and there are two basic stories in this novel, one the history of Papá James, Nenén, and their times and the other the story of Lito. He merges the two stories through flashbacks, giving them equal treatment. While the novel has shock value, it is without doubt an educational and humanizing experience; there is nothing more pressing, the author seems to imply, than educating the public to the urgency for recognition of the existence, contributions, and needs of the *chombo* in Panama.

In *Afroexiliados*, Cubena continues his pedagogical campaign and his timely portrayal of contemporary and historical black consciousness. Just as *Chombo* unfolded against the background of the Torrijos-Carter treaty negotiations, the contemporary portion of his second novel is set against the background of the first Duran-Leonard fight and the Atlanta child murders. The novel opens, however, with the author returning to and enlarging on his account of the first slave crossing and of the initial uprooting of the first "Afro exiles." In *Chombo*, Cubena's most moving pages described the slave crossing in retrospect, with its "white horrors." His second novel starts out chronologically as a historical work, tracing the plight and mistreatment of the first generation of his ancestors, the first victims of the slave trade from Africa to the New World.

In the opening chapter, which makes up the bulk of the manuscript, we witness the unease and anxiety of slave traders who fear rebellion from below by those "chained African slaves buried down in the dark and sickening hold of the ships."[4] Plotters on board, Cubena tells us, included young black women who when raped stole keys to free black males from chains. These violated women communicated information to the men below through songs and hand claps which their drunken captors mistakenly thought were "simply a show of happy gratitude *post coitum*" (p. 41). Cubena's account of slave rebellion on board ship is fascinating. He explores, as well, the depravity and criminal tendencies of those involved in the slave trade by concentrating on the career and exploits of Bartolomé Arias, whose aliases Bartolomé Ladrón ("Thief") and Bartolomé Matanegros ("Killer of Blacks") accurately reflect the character of this principal antagonist in *Afroexiliados*. By reducing all of the "deep hatred" toward blacks to this one character, the author is able to symbolize many who feared "black vengeance," which black rebellions everywhere—in Mexico, Brazil, Santo Domingo, Colombia, Haiti, Jamaica, Honduras, Venezuela—have legitimized. More than half of the manuscript is devoted to this European prototype haunted by guilt and fear.

Cubena passes through the slave period and jumps to our time to focus on more recent hardships of descendants of "great Mother Africa in the New World" (p. 8). Cubena is in a hurry to tell his story and the middle chapters are more sketched than developed. Their fleeting nature whets the appetite for more of this fascinating account that moves from Africa to the high seas to Panama and to Jamaica and back. At times, Cubena is a staccato storyteller, an action narrator whose spellbinding narration is held together and forwarded with an accumulation of "the following," "immediately after," "what's more," "and if that's not enough," and "and on top of that"; he uses these links whether he is narrating a slave rebellion, a ritual dance, a voodoo ceremony, or acts of cruelty. A problem perhaps with this second novel is that its epic sweep is truncated: it is not as ambitious, as we shall see, as Zapata Olivella's *Changó, el gran putas*. On the other hand, what Cubena's story loses in breadth it gains in intensity even though the succinct narration at times does leave the reader feeling cheated.

Despite the brevity of his two novels, however, the author can claim the same purpose as *Changó* and Alex Haley's *Roots*, but in a specifically Panamanian setting. Cubena researched his own roots for *Afroexiliados*, as he did for *Chombo,* and he continues to pay homage to blacks, particularly those who have been close to him personally. We expect to see something of *Roots* in his trilogy because the story of blacks uprooted and enslaved is basically the same all over: the amputation of limbs in runaway slaves, for example, was not limited to North America. Comparison with *Roots,* then, is inevitable, but Cubena broadens our understanding of the black experience in the New World through the Afro-Hispanic and West Indian slant he gives his novels. Cubena is an educator, and broadening our understanding is the educational purpose his books serve. *Afroexiliados* continues the lessons in black history begun in *Chombo.* Cubena does not simply list black heroes and black achievements; he works them into his narrative so that history and Latin American literature are made to reflect a black perspective often lacking.

Cubena is a courageous writer with strong convictions. Though writing hundreds of years after events, he writes with the rage and indignation of an eyewitness. To read Cubena's novels is to travel a constant journey through ethnic memory; he does not forget, and he does his homework. The humanistic power of his narration is such that his memory serves to make people better; no one can get worse than the antagonists depicted in his novels. Cubena has tried to give a human dimension to the slave crossing while at the same time treating the trade as the systematic, inhuman, and lucrative business it was. The story of the slave trade is an old one told many times, but Cubena returns to it because it is a story he is determined to set right.

Cubena does not plead for human decency: he shocks the reader into humanistic understanding through *tremendista* description, which is as powerful in his second novel as in his first. When he describes how, under the force of violent storms, "the shackles, the iron rings, and the chains brutally rip arms and legs off black slaves" (p. 25), or how "Blacks with their throats cut flayed about like epileptics in pools of their own blood" (p. 29), or when he speaks of the "stench of the dead slaves whose bodies were in an advanced state of decomposition" (p. 38), we know that history must never repeat itself.

The humanistic and educational purpose of Cubena's work, it bears repeating, is simply to make people better, especially in what he calls "my Panama." The author's hope for a better world seems to be epitomized in the example of Nenén and Papá James, who were "friends of *tout le monde*" (p. 101). "*Yes, indeed, everybody* was welcome in the home of Nenén and Papá James: Blacks and Indians, *West Indians* . . . Catholics, *rich and poor* alike . . . There was no discrimination in the hearts of those generous West Indians" (p. 104). By paying homage to Papá James and to Nenén, "*the nice lady* who raised *more than* a dozen orphans" (p. 104), Cubena leaves little doubt who our role models should be.

These first two volumes of Cubena's projected trilogy are novels of black consciousness, of *chombo* consciousness. Cubena advises blacks to educate themselves and to unite, but there is little of the advanced political awareness we find in the recent fiction of Nelson Estupiñán Bass. Perhaps that is how it should be if we view the Afro-Panamanian's novels as first steps toward black pride and race awareness. Cubena has paid artistic homage to his own black experience and that of others who have had a hand in his formation. There are many black "heroes" whose sufferings and self-sacrifices need be known, and Cubena immortalizes in print his story of Papá James and Nenén. Though seemingly an invitation to hatred, his novels are really explanations or justifications of the feelings of rage he believes blacks should feel toward racism and racial discrimination. *Chombo* and *Afroexiliados* are pleas for understanding if whites, and particularly *gringos*, are to ward off rebellion from below. This feeling is explicitly expressed in *Chombo* when Lito says, "If I were white each night before going to bed I would worry and wonder if Blacks have learned to hate like Whites."[5]

Cubena's insistence on recognition of the *chombo* presence in Panama, then, is very much consistent with the new stage of literary Americanism in which blacks claim—as Nicolás Guillén has done in Cuba and Nelson Estupiñán Bass in Ecuador—rightful identification with their new-world countries. What this Afro-Panamanian insists on, however, is not racial assimilation or *mestizaje* but *heterogeneidad*, and in this sense Cubena decomes one of the strongest supporters of Cornejo Polar's ethnohumanistic theory of heterogeneity which would allow for the retention and recognition of one's African identity, but in a new-world setting. Cubena's novels, like his poetry and his stories, reject the white aesthetic by reversing time-honored symbols that have long associated blackness with the lowest order.

It has not been easy for Cubena to resolve the problem of identity confronting the *chombo* or the Afro-Caribbean in Panama whose Anglo background, religion, and skin color set them apart. But while Cubena is concerned with restoring balance to Latin America, he also wants to find America's "true voice," one that would give a different frame of reference to the new-world continent. Cubena's concern is racial, national, and continental, and while he can only lament, resent, and rhetorically address past issues, he can and does approach present accomplishments by blacks positively and with a great deal of pride. There is a rage in Wilson's work, and anger over the exclusion of the Afro-Caribbean in Panama from Panamanian citizenship. This reluctance in Panama to associate the Afro-Caribbean with national identity drove Wilson closer to a wider racial identity and solidarity with other blacks in Latin America and throughout the world.

The core of Cubena's novels, as for his poetry and *cuentos,* is the suggestion that the dominance white Panamanians have exerted over blacks and Indians in Panama is undeserved, and he indicates this very clearly "by attributing to all his white characters flagrant personal and social defects."[6] In restoring balance Cubena reverses symbols and allows the black to win sometimes while showing that white is not always right. His ultimate goal above and beyond racial and national identity, however, is really the same as that of Nicolás Guillén and other black writers in Latin America: to establish "the priority of the human being over and above his ethnic and national affiliation."[7] This goal, Cubena and most of them seem to agree, is obtainable only after all categories of people are first accorded equally the status of full human beings.

Blackness and Beyond

Wilson's novels are powerful and Duncan's innovative, but for a radical narrative approach to fiction we have to turn to the last five novels of Nelson Estupiñán Bass: *Senderos brillantes* (1974), *Las puertas del verano*

(1978), *Toque de queda* (1978), *Bajo el cielo nublado* (1981) and *El crepúsculo* (1984). These novels show the author's adeptness with technical experimentation, but Estupiñán Bass's racial, humanistic, and social vision of Latin American reality is rarely out of view. Estupiñán Bass is a black author committed to literary Americanism and to artistic achievement. His work can either illustrate humanistic intent without abandoning style or stylistic and technical experimentation without abandoning humanism. Whatever the approach, the conclusion is the same: the correlation between artistic and social commitment is very close in his recent work.

Even before his experimental cycle, Nelson Estupiñán Bass had already established a solid reputation as a poet and novelist of revolution. His first novel, *Cuando los guayacanes florecían* (1954), for example, is an account of the Concha revolution in Esmeraldas, his native province. His second novel, *El paraíso* (1958), focuses on a revolution against oppressive officials in his province. His third novel, *El último río (1966), is a tour de force* of sociopolitical and psychological fiction. The foreign intervention broached in this novel points to the fuller exploration of this problem he undertakes eight years later in *Senderos brillantes,* the first of his five recent novels, all of which continue his interest in revolution, black protest, and what he has called man's true liberty. His additional interest in revolutionary techniques, in the art of novel writing, however, sets his five recent novels off from his earlier ones.

The lyric, utopian, and highly imaginative quality of *Senderos brillantes* is conveyed through the use of various experimental techniques, among them the inclusion of correspondence and the adoption of a second voice that acts as chorus-witness and participant, often fragmenting into multiple voices. Other narrative signatures include the absence of punctuation, accent marks, and capitalization, and the interruption of chapters: some are headed with reverse numbering, while alternating chapters are identified by letters. Sections printed side by side in columns graphically illustrate parallel activity in the novel, which ends as a war for liberation is getting under way. In his account of the "imaginary" island of Calamares the most fascinating character is black Medardo, who practices black magic, employs a truth serum, and has the "power" to turn white people into blacks. Estupiñán Bass agrees that Medardo is "the most fascinating character in the novel and I have sketched him with love and with deep affection."[8]

Estupiñán Bass has always made overbearing and pompous public officials cut ridiculous and therefore humorous figures in his novels. Humor is one of the author's strongest assets, and in *Senderos brillantes*, he puts it to effective use, for example, in his characterization of President Barragán, who suffers from three *manías* that typecast any leader who relies on "cosmetics" to hide the truth from the populace. The president suffers from *fotomanía*, a consequence of having flooded newspapers with photographs of himself taken in a hospital bed, pictures designed to show the "magnificent quality and efficiency of hospital care."[9] Sick people avoid these facilities, however, because in reality the hospitals lack beds, medicine, and food. The president also suffers an attack of *danzomanía*, from having on his travels to constantly attend dances to pretend that all was well and festive. And he suffers from *televisomanía*. Having been convinced by his associates of his striking similarity to a famous movie star, the president appears on television three or four times a week "to announce trivial matters" (p. 243)— while deferring to his ministers the announcement of such things as currency devaluation and the subsequent inflation.

The author capitalizes on his humor very early in *Senderos brillantes* in a tongue-in-cheek "recipe" his "other I" suggests for a writer who wishes to attain immediate worldwide literary success. No self-respecting writer would follow this advice, even though it would radicalize literary expression. His eight-point plan (p. 243) for world acclaim is the following:

1. Write titles backward, which some readers would take to be an invention "comparable to the invention of the wheel," one that would have "countless imitators the world over."

2. Print words upside down so that readers have to stand on their heads to read, "since a large part of the world already goes about that way anyway."

3. Fill work with obscene words to liven it up and to make the impotent reader feel young.

4. Write on every other line and someone "thinking this a new invention will help you to get a patent on it."

5. Do not mention misery and poverty. Write that everything is just fine "in order to be a candidate for the universal literary prize for lying."

6. Print each word with a different color since it is common knowledge that "each term has its own color."

7. Use eye-catching paper so that readers will not fall asleep reading it.

8. Write the novel with another voice, one that does not respect grammatical conventions.

Estupiñán Bass's experiments are hardly as radical as these. He does use the "other voice" which dispenses with grammatical convention, but his other revolutionary techniques are mild compared to most of these intentionally humorous suggestions, which, in effect, poke fun at the absurd extremes some experimental novelists go in their search for the new and for universal acclaim. Some of Estupiñán Bass's technical innovations in *Senderos brillantes* are distracting, but one of his major innovations, namely, his use of the "other I" in combination on another level with traditional dialogue, is a successful attempt to give his story multiple perspectives while at the same time dispensing with background details in the straight narrative flow. Estupiñán Bass tries to again remove background information from the traditional narrative in *Las puertas del verano,* but he gives it an entirely new look in this second of his five experimental novels.

Las puertas del verano opens with the tall tales of Don Argandoña, a character almost as fascinating as Medardo, the black pivotal figure in *Senderos brillantes.* Don Argandoña's tales, which he relates to two cousins about to undertake a journey to the coast to sell their wares, are so unbelievable the reader—and his listeners—are reluctant to take him seriously. But he does introduce us to two cities, Casacar and Chontalvi, one totally white and the other where the color white is anathema. In Chontalvi, controlled by blacks, milk, for example, is red and sugar green. Such imaginative visions enrich the author's humor and reverse symbols in the manner of Nicolás Guillén and Cubena. They underscore, as well, the radical consciousness that is always present in Estupiñán Bass's novels. Even the Hitler clones or replicas that appear toward the end of the novel are further manifestations of the author's strong and consistent opposition to the dangers inherent in a belief in master or super races.

The new look in *Las puertas del verano,* though, has more to do with the way the author tells the story than with the story itself, for here as in *Senderos brillantes* Estupiñán Bass operates on two different levels that periodically merge in each of the three parts of the novel, which the author himself has advised us how to read: "First read the odd numbered pages of the first part up to page 66, then the even numbered pages, and from page 67 on, you can read them in order. Do the same with parts II and III."[10] The two levels are not only separate mechanically; they are also very different in kind. On one level we have, as in *Senderos brillantes,* traditional narration with dialogue, what we can call the public actions and activities of the characters. On the other, we have their private and confidential history. This second level allows the author "to depart from traditional novel forms"; here, he narrates through what can be called official documentation.

Senderos brillantes has the "other voice" and letters. *Las puertas del verano* includes letters as well, but in addition the author incorporates a series of "official" fact sheets, reports, and questionnaires to augment the private and confidential background material on his characters that he shares with the readers. This official documentation, in a sense Secret Service reports, is designed to introduce alphabetically "real people" from whom the characters are drawn. Once again Estupiñán Bass removes from the narrative stream background description that normally contributes to characterizations so that we can see the characters acting out their roles more quickly and more directly. Though they might seem so at first, these fact sheets, reports, letters, and questionnaires are not extraneous. We soon realize they deal with the same characters acting out roles on the other level in the novel.

This use of official documentation, or "officialese" (as Mario Vargas Llosa's use of similar devices in his *Pantaleón y las visitadoras* has been called),[11] does indeed remind us of the Peruvian author's acclaimed novel, which has been translated into English as *Captain Pantoja and the*

Secret Service. But if this second experimental novel of Estupiñán Bass reminds us of Vargas Llosa, his third, *Toque de queda,* is reminiscent of Miguel Angel Asturias's *El señor presidente* in theme, as well as in structure and technique. In his anti-Fascist work, Estupiñán Bass explores the effects of dictatorship on the populace by giving, through a vivid cross-section of narrative voices, an inside view of those who are victimized by the totalitarian governments.

One of these voices defines a "jefe supremo" in language even a child can understand:

// daddy what is a supreme head / a civilian or a military man who not being able to become president of the country through the election process seizes the office by force or through the back door as we sometimes say / how long is he in power / for as long as he can or until he fills his pockets with money or until those who helped put him there kick him out / why / because others also want to get rich / do the supreme heads get rich / when they leave office they are millionaires / daddy why don't you do that / because I wasn't born to be a tyrant or a thief and to become either would disgrace our whole family / but daddy we would be able to buy so many things we don't have like a television / it's better to be poor than to have people pointing at you or talking about you behind your back or calling you a son of a . . .//[12]

In *Toque de queda* Estupiñán Bass not only shows guerilla opposition to Fascist dictatorship (p. 67); his novel also relates internal power struggles among the "white-collar thieves" (*ladrones encorbatadas*) themselves. Part of the interest in the novel is generated by the uncertainty about which leader will emerge or remain "el jefe supremo," a title that represents a step up in repressive power from "el excelentísimo señor presidente." The winner in this internal power struggle announces his victory in the following speech, which shows Estupiñán Bass's skill in parodying political rhetoric, or the empty presidential address:

As our heroic armed forces and the entire citizenry of this country are my witnesses let it be known far and wide that I have harbored no political ambitions and that my professional and private conduct has been inspired solely by modesty and an honesty beyond reproach but there are times when the nation lying prostrate and torn asunder with grief by countless upheavals sends out an anguished cry to its best sons to rise up in anger and come forward and with good diagnosis and an even better treatment to take over the reins of government and lead it victoriously down the paths of moral, intellectual, economic and spiritual progress and material growth to not respond to the clamors of the people of this sick nation in these historic moments when the country from north to south and from east to west and all points in between is about to succumb to demagogy and anarchy would be an injurious crime which generations present future and beyond would condemn in the harshest terms it is for this reason beloved citizens that conscious of my grave responsibility and inspired by the divine light of our benefactor and supported by our legendary armed forces and the wise judgement of the country who have seen in my humble and peaceful person the one citizen who because of his civic virtues is the most logical one to bring the country out of this dismal and dangerous undertaking it finds itself in I have resolved to leave behind the delightful tranquility of my sacred home to accept the patriotic duty imposed on me and to make this sacrifice by taking in my hands the reins of our tormented nation . . . I warn the country with the frankness that characterizes my every act that my government will be truly unyielding and will wage war without quarter against international communism . . . and I will stamp out that sick ideology that has taken hold in some of the tired and worn out minds of our people . . . //

// what do you think Joe / pure bla bla bla the same foolish ramblings as the other one / . . . (p. 61–62)

The curfew in the novel, which also gives the work its name, was imposed "on the pretext of catching communists" (p. 21) as they are in the forefront of the guerilla war waged against the Fascist dictatorship. But the strongest opposition comes from "the Black Star," the guerilla group made up of the "six brave Blacks" who lead the fight. There is race pride in the novel even though the six black freedom fighters put their heroism to test for the collective good. The black pride of these characters pushes them toward opposition: "Remember, we are black and none of these recent governments loves black people" (p. 18). Again: "I wear my color with pride because by God I am black and I'll say it anywhere" (p. 12). The relationship is clear between the author's race pride and his opposition to racist/Fascist governments.

Estupiñán Bass deals more with heroism in the face of fear than with fear of the dictator, the latter a basic theme in Asturias's *El señor presi-*

dente. Asturias shows what happens when a dictatorship is tolerated, and Estupiñán Bass how to deal with it. Both show the psychological impact of life under a dictatorship. Each novel achieves aesthetic value through an original approach to the subject. In addition, *Toque de queda's* form recalls *El señor presidente* as well. As in Asturias's novel there is a definite time period involved in *Toque de queda*. The first part of *El señor presidente* takes place in three days, the second in four days, and the last in weeks, months, and years. *Toque de queda*, a good example of thematics determining technique, structure, and style, takes the shape and form of the curfew in force: the novel is divided not into chapters but according to the hours of the curfew—from 7:00 P.M. to 5:00 A.M.—beginning with the first chapter or hour (7:00–8:00 P.M.) and ending with the last chapter or hour (4:00–5:00 A.M.).

Toque de queda is narrated through a series of voices and in a sense seems to be an updated version of a chapter from *El señor presidente*, where Asturias uses a similar technique. But even within these multiple voices Estupiñán Bass, as in *Senderos brillantes* and *Las puertas del verano*, again, utilizes two narrative levels: one a media level complete with newspaper headlines and radio broadcasts that carry, for example, presidential decrees, speeches, and military laws prohibiting such "subversive" activities as protest songs and poetry, and the other a private level where we see lives affected by those public media announcements. A radio broadcast, which gives us the meaning of the title, is very useful in providing background and in filling in information that forwards the action.

Whatever the level, whether public or private, Estupiñán Bass economizes his expression by eliminating punctuation. The author returns to the run-on sentence, devoid of punctuation, used in *Senderos brillantes*, but he divides *Toque de queda* into paragraphs with occasional slashes between breath groups. Each paragraph or voice for the most part begins *in medias res* and is preceded and followed by ellipsis points to better suggest conversations overheard. This technique gives the short novel a rapid-fire, fast-paced, and urgent flavor. Estupiñán Bass uses two narrative levels in *Toque de queda*, but unlike the superimposed narrative strands in his first two experimental novels, these two levels have the same narrative style, one that is appropriate to the accelerated pace of the activity during the twenty-four-hour curfew period, which included the two *golpes de estado* as well as the internal power struggles and a revolution.

Economy of expression resulting in heightened intensity reaches maximum effectiveness in the following gang-rape scene where style is very much at the service of that desired intensity:

// . . . don't treat me badly let me go for God's sake I am just a child / don't grab my hand sweetie just be still so I won't hurt you look I like you / no let me go / be quiet don't attract attention / don't put your hand over my mouth don't tear my dress / then stop resisting sweet thing / I am not a woman of the streets don't do it here / you want me to take you to a rooming house / I don't know about those things yet / I'm going to teach you cutie don't be bad like me don't you see I like you / don't tear my dress my head is bleeding from this rock you've got me against / it's not my fault I keep telling you to lie still but you keep carrying on / I have a boyfriend . . . we are going to get mar- ried . . . I told him I was a virgin / dammit I'm losing my patience with you are you going to let me . . . / no no don't tear my stockings / open your legs . . . / don't tear my / sweet vir / brassiere / gin / don't . . . bit me / no / no / yes you whore . . . / don't cut me . . . / take off your / ay ay ay I'm bleed / brassiere / ing / and open up / what a fix to be shut up in this store . . . and not being able to go out and kick hell out of that guy / ay / you want another nick / nonono do what you want don't cut me again . . . don't bite my breasts for God's sake what will I tell my boyfriend when he sees them . . . / what's up Raoul / you want this bitch sure / no for God's sake no I can't be passed around like that have pity can't you see I'm bleeding / be quiet / take those rags off and . . . / damn how I wish I could get out of here and help that poor girl / you want another nick / no no just go ahead / hurry up Jacinto I think some people are coming / kiss me you sweet little . . . // (Pp. 62–63)

The interplay of voices that narrate parallel or simultaneous action is reduced to its lowest terms in this scene where words themselves are cut up, suspended, and taken over by contrapuntal utterances. The result is not dehumanization or incomprehension but an intense dramatization of abusive disregard for the human and sexual rights of others.

The reader has to work a little harder to read *Toque de queda* because the divisions are less mechanical than in Estupiñán Bass's other recent fiction. But the run-on narrative flow gives this novel a powerful immediacy not found in the others. This is not to say that artistic achievement is lacking in *Senderos brillantes, Las puertas del verano, Bajo el cielo nublado,* and *El crepúsculo* only that in *Toque de queda* the reader enters a fictional world whose duration—like our reading of the novel itself—we know will come to an end when the curfew is lifted. Given the dusk-to-dawn curfew, one can only applaud the narrative style the author chose to "enforce" it. Within the limited time set by the curfew, Estupiñán Bass achieves maximum narrative activity with his nonstop flood of words. *Toque de queda,* I repeat, is a good example of thematics determining technique, structure, and style.

In all of his recent fiction Estupiñán Bass shows that narration should unfold on different levels and that multiple voices relating the same story from different perspectives can express all levels of society. The author's concern with point of view is especially evident in *Bajo el cielo nublado,* the fourth in his recent experimental cycle. Here Estupiñán Bass continues his refreshing approach to narration by having natural and environmental resources themselves relate much of the story. Objective narration does not become a dehumanizing device; rather, by humanizing these support systems the author modernizes his message. Those elements most directly affected by exploitation and spoliation not only give multiple perspectives and insights to his story; they also bear witness to the sellout of the government to foreign powers. First in the long prologue and again the the epilogue, nature personified presents the human story and then passes judgment on those responsible for the country's ruin. Natural and environmental resources not only act as chorus-witnesses to their own destruction; being the real victims, they are as well quick to express their displeasure firsthand.

As narrative devices "things" react to events and provide background information useful to our understanding. The novel proper takes place in two parts (there are no chapters) sandwiched between the prologue and epilogue. Environmental structures in the prologue again narrate in the epilogue, but in reverse order. The last voice we hear in the prologue before the story proper begins is the sky, which in prepollution days was clear and uncontaminated. The first voice we hear in the epilogue is this same sky now "nublado" or darkened with the smoke-filled cloud of pollution. Nelson Estupiñán Bass's environmental concern makes his novel timely in the ecological sense: any equally concerned reader anywhere can identify with the lament of the sea, the last environmental voice we hear: "How can I not get sick if, through exhaust outlets which the company doesn't bother to close, pipes pump 100,000 barrels of crude oil a year in my waters! If that is not enough tankers smear my face with waste products daily . . . I get mad when these tankers cast anchor in my waters . . . and I am even more furious when the river cannot help but dump its waste in me."[13]

This voice of the sea not only laments environmental ruin; it touches as well on other aspects of the Era Petrolera in Ecuador. In *Senderos brillantes* Estupiñán Bass already had focused on the increasing importance of Ecuadorian oil in the world market. In *Bajo el cielo nublado* he returns to this theme with a vengeance. Suspecting that oil production would bring pollution and environmental ruin, he is also aware that the Era Petrolera would mean only that the rich would get richer and the poor poorer. Estupiñán Bass does not oppose progress, only a system where the poor suffer while the well-off benefit in complicity with foreign powers.

Estupiñán Bass is a debater, and much like the *contrapunteos* in his popular poetry, his novels often debate issues that affect the well-being and future direction of his people, his province, and his country. *Bajo el cielo nublado* is just such a debate, and a highly imaginative one, on the advantages and disadvantages an oil refinery would bring to his "Provincia Verde"—the issue, of course, being whether such an installation would bring progress and jobs ("trabajo honrado y dinero a montones") or simply high hopes and smog. Overriding all of his concerns, perhaps, is the question of foreign domination and exploitation. In this novel the author, in the best tradition of literary Americanism, continues to staunchly defend national culture and is especially adamant about the need for decolonialization. *Bajo el cielo nublado* is a strong protest against dependency and foreign intervention, and the author enlivens his protest with the creation of Roque Quintero, an Ecuadorian who forms alliances with foreign powers and sells out himself and his country. A ridiculous character, Quintero becomes a pathetic symbol of the practices and attitudes Estupiñán Bass attacks.

If there is any one recurring protagonist in the novel, it is Roque Quintero. Estupiñán Bass has often attacked the brainwashed black who wants to be white, and he does it again in this novel with characters who hate "that damned color." In the person of Roque Quintero, however, the author goes beyond the rejection of color to create a character who also rejects his country and his Hispanic heritage. Roque Quintero is the ultimate absurdity, namely, a Hispanic "Gringoized Mulatto." This "Gringoized Esmeraldan" who loves everything "Made in the U.S.A." went to the United States, turned his hair blond, became a "nationalized Yanqui," changed his name to Rock King, and returned to his province to exploit it—and he returned speaking a crazy language that "sounds like English."

Roque Quintero, now Rock King, explains his name change:

Yes, en los *iunait Esteits mí* estuvo obligado
cambiag nombe . . . no *usag long neims* . . .
allá todo *fast* . . . *taim is mony* . . . *nombes cogtos*
. . . *du iu ¿understand?* . . . *fog* eso *llamagme Rock King*
. . . *abebiatuga of* Roque *Quintego* . . .

¡Dad is! Piur inglish . . . mucho *mejog*
que Roque *Quintego* . . . *inglish supeguiog in al*
a *espanish* . . . *espanish* lengua baja . . .
pobe in *al.* (p. 103)

Through humor, Nelson Estupiñán Bass has always made his targets cut ridiculous figures, and here more than ever because what Quintero does and says are as absurd as the fractured language he uses. Quintero is the primary target in the novel, but there are other misguided characters who sell out their race, their culture, or their country. There are other would-be or "nationalized" Yankees—Quintero's brother, for example. There is the black woman who dreams of being white and whose one obsession is to become "the wife of a mister" and thereby the happiest woman in the world. This same woman speaks with "a fake Spanish accent" and hates everything black, including "that damned marimba music."

The marimba as narrative voice ridicules this woman's "crazy desire to marry a Gringo" and her campaign to have the marimba and "all that damned African music abolished all over the Province" (p. 227). Her campaign meets with some success since, as the marimba laments, "young people do not like my music; they prefer, unfortunately, North American music" (p. 227). The marimba voice in the novel is an important one because it is the spokesman for the true vernacular. In a passage strongly reminiscent of Nicolás Guillén in *West Indies, Ltd.*, the marimba voice speaks:

I laugh at those so-called "Typical Native Groups" . . . that perform on street corners and beg for handouts and serenade rich folk hoping they'll throw them some coins or a bottle of drink. How demeaning! I also laugh at groups that go to Guayaquil and Quito to present what they call "native art." These guys are fakes and wheeler dealers and they don't know anything except how to deceive people in those cities. They don't know anything about the true art of the people of Esmeraldas . . . I think all of them are jokes" (P. 228)

In a sense, *Bajo el cielo nublado* is Nelson Estupiñán Bass's *West Indies, Ltd.* and the two works are nowhere better paralleled than in the above paragraph because it reflects the same mad scramble to put one's national identity aside that Nicolás Guillén was attacking in the 1930s. Guillén's use of English as a sarcastic literary tool comes of age in his *West Indies, Ltd.* just as Estupiñán Bass's does in his recent Ecuadorian novel. Both works stand out for their consciousness raising, as much cultural and racial as national and political. Just as Guillén rejected "dollar diplomacy," Estupiñán Bass preaches common sense in the pursuit of the "hard-to-get dollar." Ecuadorians should not worship too blindly the new "Pagan God," this "abominable modern idol" Ecuadorian oil now represents.

Finally, in *El crepúsculo*[14] Nelson Estupiñán Bass combines his social vision with reader involvement in the creative process. Surpassing even his own recent experimental fiction, this novel, his most radical departure to date, has a "do-it-yourself" ending. By inviting the reader to finish "writing" his novel Estupiñán Bass carries his interest in narrative structure and point of view to the ultimate possible extreme. The author extends this invitation in what I consider to be part 3 of the novel (the appendix). Part 1 is made up of correspondence between characters whose identities are not immediately apparent. The first-person narration of this part contrasts with the third-person narration of part 2 where the recipient of many of the letters returns home to investigate firsthand the events discussed in the correspondence of part 1.

Much of the action in the novel takes place in a poor district where a smallpox epidemic is decimating the black population. The narrator returns home to find his city in the throes not only of this health crisis but of economic ruin as well. He also uncovers a racist plot to eliminate blacks by denying them access to vaccinations against the disease. The emotional high point of the novel is the confrontation between health officials and a black priest who, choosing between black survival and the priesthood, reveals publicly the guilt-ridden confession of a participant in the "For Whites Only" vaccination plan. *El crepúsculo* is a novel of a city in hard times dying before the onslaught of economic and health problems. Nelson Estupiñán Bass draws a forceful parallel between a city settling into a *nefasto crepúsculo* and the black race, both under siege and struggling for their very existence. As the author himself tells us, this novel, his most recent, contains some passages on the black theme written "with passion."[15]

Nelson Estupiñán Bass, like Nicolás Guillén, starts from the humanistic premise that "the best use of human activity is to alleviate human misery";[16] his role as a writer, as he sees it, is to be informed and to inform. The author has a special love for his province and for his people, and we see this affection even transferred to the nonhuman spokesmen that populate his novel. By stressing their "humanity," Estupiñán Bass's experiments with point of view continue to be innovative and his powers of imagination strong. Though he abandons the traditional novel, his targets and his humanistic vision have always remained the same.

In these five new novels the author's narrative technique changed, but not his messages or his vision. He continues in his recent fiction to denounce the "sellouts" (the "vende-patrias") and the "El señor presidente" types whom he assails for their dishonesty, immorality, and greed. By continually denouncing Fascist governments that dehumanize man, Estupiñán Bass's themes have remained constant. In the final analysis, his books, like those of Mario Vargas Llosa, deal for the most part with authoritarianism. Vargas Llosa himself has said that in the majority of Latin American countries the fundamental problem is authoritarianism, or military dictatorship. As such, "a novel or motion picture that refers to this very problem is one which is deeply rooted in the current problems of Latin America."[17]

Estupiñán Bass is extremely protective of Latin American life and culture; defending his country is synonymous with rejecting imported and homegrown racism, opposing foreign influence, and denouncing corrupt dictatorships. In his novels those who fight against tyranny and political sellout are not "against the country, only against those who govern badly."[18] To Estupiñán Bass true liberty means "everyone doing what he or she pleases, as long as you don't hurt anyone."[19] To guarantee this liberty Estupiñán Bass suggests that the time has passed for the "inactive singing of protest songs."[20] Like Miguel Angel Asturias, he insists that protest must be taken out of the sanctuary of university walls and into the streets.

Estupiñán Bass populates his novels with blacks, whites and Indians. As if to underscore Fernández Retamar's position that barbarism does not reside in the ethnic peoples of America but rather among the representatives (*gorilas,* he calls them) of racist/Fascist governments, Estupiñán Bass highlights the black Hispanic model in his works. We saw this tendency in his popular poetry where the black voice of Alberto Cuabú becomes "the great new *Mandinga,*" the new American voice, one that acts as a modern black everyman speaking for Latin America and for the Third World. The author hinted at the role model blacks play in *Canto negro por la luz* (1954), an earlier volume of erudite poetry. In *Senderos brillantes* Medardo's presence is strong, as are his "magical powers." The "six brave Blacks" led the revolution against the racist/ Fascist dictatorship in *Toque de queda.* In *Las puertas del verano* the black village Chontalvi is famous for its resistance against white aggression. In

Bajo el cielo nublado, Nelson Estupiñán Bass again is adamant in his defense of black culture in Esmeraldas, and the black priest is really the
hero in *El crepúsculo.* But like Nicolás Guillén, he joins in solidarity with
anyone who opposes tyranny; the implication, however, is clear: blacks
have the most to lose in a racist dictatorship. In short, Nelson Estupiñán
Bass, like his Central American and other black Hispanic colleagues,
continues to press for human rights and freedoms in his efforts to give
ethnic balance to Latin American literature.

Negridumbre *and the "Humanly Real"*

This same quest for authenticity is furthered by Jorge Artel, Juan Zapata
Olivella, and by Manuel Zapata Olivella in Colombia. Like Nelson Estupiñán Bass, Jorge Artel is also a poet, but one who is very much at
ease in the novel form. Artel narrates with a fluidity that at times es-
capes Juan Zapata Olivella, another contemporary black poet who is
beginning to try his hand at novel writing. In Artel's *No es la muerte, es el
morir*[21] (1979) words flow simply and unpretentiously in an unexpect-
edly readable style, considering that this is a poet writing prose. Again
like Nelson Estupiñán Bass, Artel develops themes of heroism, solidarity, revolutionary consciousness, and guerrilla warfare. Artel focuses
on the role of the clergy in the struggle against man's inhumanity to
man. His primary target: a *latifundismo* (landownership system) that is
both *antihumano* and *criminal.* The author is not hysterical in his quest
for human justice; his characters, however, are forceful and determined
in their struggle against the remnants of an outmoded feudal system.

In his first novel, *Historia de un joven negro*[22] (1983), Juan Zapata
Olivella is equally concerned with human justice in Colombia. The author demonstrates his awareness of blacks in early and recent history in
Latin America, the United States, and around the world, and he dedi-
cates this book to the memory of Martin Luther King, Jr. His focus is on
black freedom, and he highlights, for the most part, racism, both blatant
and subtle, in Colombia. The author builds an image of racist whites
from the first page and leaves the reader to judge who the real heroes

are: the black cadet who gives his life to save another from certain death, or the white naval academy officials who tried hard to deny him admission. Zapata Olivella's concern with black humanity continues in his second novel, *Pisando el camino de ébano*[23] (1984), which again characterizes blacks denied access in present-day Colombia, this time to medical school. Juan Zapata Olivella's novels expose the myth of racial equality in Colombia as a falsehood perpetuated by the government and its public officials.

The right to dream and to aspire is a strong motivating force in Zapata Olivella's work. Believing that man's spiritual growth has not kept pace with scientific progress, the author focuses on the indomitable human spirit and the need to achieve. Though inspired by such black role models as Martín de Porres, Martin Luther King, Jr., Langston Hughes, and Booker T. Washington, Juan Zapata Olivella creates role models of his own in his literature, which is, in turn, patterned on his own not inconsiderable accomplishments. The ebony path blacks walk is not always just physical. His black protagonist journeys through Central America, as the author himself had done, and he has many racist encounters before reaching his destination, the United States. But his greatest realization along the way is that to walk the ebony path is to tread a very thin line, where one is "completely alone with one's thoughts and one's *"negridumbre"* (p. 42).

Juan Zapata Olivella conveys state of mind very well, and he explores human reactions to human problems. His young black heroes are educated and upwardly mobile. As his black protagonist journeys toward the United States, the Afro-Colombian author takes the reader of today through the black Hispanic world with a refreshing candor. The black protagonists of both his novels are proud, assertive examples of black manhood who demand opportunity as they seek to develop their human potential to the fullest. His protagonists/heroes never forget who they are as they travel the ebony path, nor do they allow the reader to forget that for Colombia to try to put on a white face to the world is to lose sight of the "essence of the humanly real" (p. 11) in that Latin American country. Manuel Zapata Olivella has done the same thing, but on a much larger scale, in his big new novel *Changó, el gran putas*.

Chapter Six

The
Shango
Saga

If you have the patience to listen I can talk for a thousand and one days about the great epic history of my people.

—The *Babaloa*,
in *Changó, el gran putas*

Journey to Commitment

Nowhere are black literature and humanism better illustrated than in the work of the Afro-Colombian Manuel Zapata Olivella, whose novels begin with the lives of black people and reach out to all humanity. The culmination of his humanistic perspective to date is exemplified, as we shall see, by his *Changó, el gran putas* (1983). But before discussing Zapata Olivella's newest novel I would like to trace the origin and growth of that perspective by looking at one of the Colombian author's first works, published exactly thirty years earlier: *He visto la noche.*[1] This little book regrettably has been overlooked in our classrooms. Though it will be overshadowed by the author's much more ambitious *Changó, el gran putas*, it is nevertheless significant because it represents an inside view of black life in the United States, but seen from the perspective of a black who comes from outside that country. This book should be better known, since it reflects very well Zapata Olivella's response to the most basic of humanistic questions: Whom should literature help?

He visto la noche falls in the category of black autobiographical literature written by black Hispanic writers who come to the United States and write about their experiences here, whether in straight autobiographical accounts or in thinly disguised fiction. Some of the works, for example, of Carlos Guillermo Wilson, the Afro-Panamanian author, also fit this category. Though born in Panama City, Wilson, or "Cubena," moved to the United States, received his doctorate in Hispanic languages from the University of California at Los Angeles, and addressed the U.S. experience of the black Hispanic in such stories as "La depravada," where a white *compañera* breaks off a relationship with the distinguished Dr. Cubena, much to the satisfaction of the girl's mother. Cubena is again protagonist in "La fiesta," where the author chides silly customs of some of his white American associates.

In Wilson's stories, as in his novels, whites often cut ridiculous figures. What he shows largely is that blacks from outside the United States, even intellectuals with Ph.D.'s, are viewed negatively by white society. Manuel Zapata Olivella's account of his sojourn in the United States, however, takes another direction. Both Wilson and Zapata Olivella write autobiographical literature, but two important differences override the similarities. In the first place, Wilson's autobiographical experiences are fictionalized. The protagonists of his stories are thinly disguised versions of the author. Manuel Zapata Olivella, on the other hand, writes what is in a sense a diary/travelogue, but one complete with the creative reconstruction of dialogue. Zapata Olivella is undoubtedly the star and center attraction of the adventures he narrates. Secondly, while both write eyewitness firsthand accounts of the experiences of foreign blacks in the United States, Wilson focuses on the trials and tribulations of the black in white society in the states and on the shortcomings of that society. Manuel Zapata Olivella, on the other hand, represents the black from the outside who came into the United States in search of his black brother and of the brotherhood of the black community. Zapata Olivella's travels around the United States become a black odyssey, a journey into blackness and into the racial, social, and humanistic commitment that will later characterize *Changó, el gran putas*. His Shango saga is our subject here, but it is Zapata Olivella's own black odyssey, the author's journey to commitment, that underlies his work.

In the early 1940s Manuel Zapata Olivella set out on foot from his native Colombia on a journey that would ultimately take him into the United States. He passed through Central American countries and Mexico and wrote about these pre–U.S. experiences in *Pasión vagabunda*, which he published in 1949. The literary account of his travels culminates in *He visto la noche,* written in 1946 and published in 1953, a little book that deals exclusively with his time in the United States. Zapata Olivella was a student in his last years of medical school when he started his journey, but he wanted to get away for a while to think, to accumulate life experiences, and to decide if he really wanted to go into the medical profession. He subsequently did take a degree in medicine and became a doctor, as well as a practicing psychiatrist, social anthropologist, musicologist, and writer—one of the most widely read black authors writing in Spanish today. At that time, however, he was not sure, so he took to the road to work it out in his mind.

By traveling across the United States Zapata Olivella had the same kinds of experiences as other blacks. The adventures he narrates include many instances of and encounters with racism. His book, which carries the subtitle *Las raíces de la furia negra* (*The Roots of Black Rage*), catalogs racist abuses, discrimination, and segregation. His chapter titles alone run the gamut of black experiences:

Jim Crow in Hollywood
Black Chicago
Black Baptism
Worshipper of Father Devine
Solidarity with the Unfortunate
The Forgotten Harlem
The Color Line
In K.K.K. Territory
The Struggle for Human Dignity
The Final Insult

His book tells us things about U.S. race relations we already knew. We know about "Jim Crow in Hollywood," for example, and we know about segregated buses, Zapata Olivella's main mode of transportation when he was in the United States in the 1940s. The main interest here is what his book tells us about race and the ethnic experience of a black from a different milieu and about the alliance and cooperation he sought and found in the black community. We know his experiences but we learn his reaction to them and witness his personal growth and development as a black and as a committed writer.

Many of the experiences the author encountered in the United States reinforced the pride in blackness he came with: "Me sentí orgulloso de ser negro" (I felt proud of being a Black) is a phrase often repeated. Each racist abuse he was subjected to made him hold his head higher. Analyzing his adventures Manuel Zapata Olivella saw that much of the racism at the time was retaliation by white racists to his refusal to bow. He quickly understood that the humiliation of blacks, especially black intellectuals like himself, was their aim.

In his chapter "Black Chicago" Zapata Olivella, the budding journalist, narrates his visit to that city with a plan he hoped to have published in the black press. This plan, which he outlined in a series of articles, called for a common front for addressing wrongs throughout the Americas, a plan that can be considered a forerunner of the Congress on Black Culture in the Americas Zapata Olivella was instrumental in bringing to Colombia in the late 1970s. At this point in his cross-country odyssey Zapata Olivella was beginning to feel an especially close affinity with blacks whose economic situation paralleled his own. Those were hard times and he was living close to a starvation level.

From black Chicago he moved on to New York where he experienced the phenomenon and the generosity of Father Devine. He also experienced the generosity of Langston Hughes, whose works he had read and whose help he was ultimately to seek. After days of hunger and nights of sleeping in subways, flophouses, and bus stations Zapata Olivella's resurrection as a writer was influenced by Langston Hughes, who rekindled his interest in writing, especially about black people. In the following passage the Colombian author describes their first meeting:

I knocked on his door hopeful that he would help me sell some articles to the black newspapers in New York. Behind this help I intended to ask of him lay hidden the deep admiration I felt for him as a man and a poet, which his stories and the few poems of his I knew had awakened in me. I found in Langston Hughes the poet much more than what my humble heart could hope for: a friend. We struck up a lively conversation as if he had known me from one of the far away ports in Africa or Europe he had visited in times past . . . My stories wakened in him some long forgotten memories, and I brought him up to date on places in South America which he had only heard about during his stay in Mexico. He got most excited when I told about some of his Mexican friends . . . and he remembered the smells of Xochimilco, the snows of Popocatepetl, the poets he knew, and the Revolution. He tried every way to help me solve my money problem; and after I tried, unsuccessfully, to translate García Lorca into English for an anthology, he found a lady who wanted to learn Spanish. My student turned out to be the wife of the black singer and actor Kenneth Spencer. All kinds of black artists, painters, writers, musicians and art critics met in his house. I attended several of these evening meetings and among that talented elite discovered the forceful leadership the black liberation struggle has . . . Langston didn't intervene too much in the wide ranging, animated but cordial discussions; he just nodded or smiled or shook his head approvingly or disapprovingly. Afterwards, he would explain to me some things I hadn't understood in moments of heated debate . . . I felt that these meetings and discussions had a strong influence on my own ideas and opened new routes for me to travel. (Pp. 126–27)

This passage is significant because it indicates how, with Langston Hughes's help, Zapata Olivella was able not only to overcome some personal difficulties but also to benefit firsthand from various discussions held among black writers and artists whose ideas about black liberation, he admits, had a profound impact on him.

Zapata Olivella's sojourn exemplifies the magnetic impact Harlem had on black Hispanics, both visitors and immigrants. In the chapter "The Forgotten Harlem," however, we see that Harlem up close was a rude awakening for the author:

The Harlem that I was witnessing was not the marvellous district the newspapers talked about. In vain I looked for little black kids dancing the "swing" on street corners and women adorned in expensive fur coats. Gone were the days when Duke Ellington attracted the white elite to the ballrooms of the Cotton Club, when Louis Armstrong played his golden trumpet before the aghast big wheels from downtown who came up under the cover of darkness. The only thing left from those days was the legend. All I could see now were anguish, bitterness and gloom on the faces of the people . . .

On Sunday mornings Harlem woke up to the laughter of children who filled the streets . . . But the sorrow of Harlem affected me. It hurt me to see the overcrowded conditions of people living on top of one another, people whose black faces despite the pretense of happiness put on for the visitors were lined with misery and grief. (Pp. 135 and 137)

As a result of meeting Langston Hughes in New York and seeing Harlem close up the "muchacho latino" got involved in the fight against prejudice and discrimination and made speeches to this effect in broken English. More importantly, he vowed to write about the human drama of "sick Harlem" and about the misfortunes of all he had seen in his travels.

Zapata Olivella makes this commitment to combat racism even before undertaking the ultimate adventure, which would be his trip through the Deep South on his way back down to Colombia. Against the advice of friends who told him horror stories about lynchings, mutilations, and other pathological manifestations of the sick doctrine of white supremacy, Zapata Olivella made his "freedom ride" south. When he first entered the United States he was reluctant to go south, but now he knew he had to test his newfound resolve to observe, experience, and write. He knew he had to experience "jimcrowism" in the Deep South firsthand. On the Greyhound trip he was tested in Washington, D.C., and points south, and each humiliating incident witnessed or suffered brought him closer in fraternity and solidarity to his black brother.

Back home in Colombia Manuel Zapata Olivella was prepared to confront human problems with a new militancy. Having himself suffered the hunger and want that undermine human dignity, the Afro-Colombian author had returned better able to appreciate the sufferings of others. On his return he continued his medical studies, but Zapata Olivella, convinced that the poor of the world drowning in their own misery were perhaps more in need than the physically ill, from that point on became a student not only of medicine but of the cancer of racism and other pathological ills of society. Racism and injustice, he realized, inflict as much pain and cause as much human suffering, for example, as an ulcer or a ruptured appendix. Through medicine and through literature he would work for the improvement of the human condition.

Zapata Olivella later wrote other stories about black life in the United States reminiscent of the civil rights movement during the highly publicized years of the 1960s. But *He visto la noche* is important for the black American reader because it bears early witness to the concerns and anxieties of black Americans in the 1940s and to the growth of black ethnic consciousness. Having seen some of this growth up close Zapata Olivella considers his account of his experiences in the United States to be an educational document of that early period in the black struggle against racism and injustice. In a sense his book is reminiscent of John Griffin's *Black Like Me*, the true account of a white man who darkened his skin so he could travel incognito through the South and experience the same hell as blacks. Griffin wanted his account to be as authentic as possible— thus the necessity to darken his skin. Zapata Olivella already had that "advantage": he did not have to "paint himself black," which makes his account even more fascinating for the North American reader.

One of the purposes, certainly one of the results, achieved in *He visto la noche* was the charting of the roots of black consciousness in the United States. The author's account as participant and as witness is educational, as is the development of his own consciousness, an awakening inspired, fortified, and reinforced by black examples and role models he encountered in the United States. In his cross-country odyssey Zapata Olivella experienced hate, hurt, and insult on a double scale—as a black and as a Hispanic—and he traces very clearly how these experiences helped mold his feelings of racial and ethnic solidarity with both groups in the United States. *He visto la noche* shows how one man's personal unity with his black brothers was strengthened. But on an even larger scale Zapata Olivella's black odyssey was a model journey from objective analysis to human commitment. In a sense, his journey to commitment symbolizes the road all black writers in Latin America have taken—not on foot, to be sure, but with the same goals in view, namely, identity with blackness and a wider humanistic concern for the welfare of all engaged in the struggle for human dignity. Zapata Olivella's journey led to *Changó, el gran putas*, but *He visto la noche* was a major step along the way.

"Soul Force," from Africa to America

In May 1983 Manuel Zapata Olivella published *Changó, el gran putas,* his long-awaited epic of the black experience in Africa and the New World. The Colombian author had not published a novel since 1964, but for most of these nineteen years he had been working on this impressive volume, undoubtedly the most ambitious black novel ever written in Spanish. More than that, *Changó, el gran putas* is a novel of the Americas, especially of those Americans who have their roots in Africa. It is a novel about "soul-force," the unbreakable courage and human spirit of Africans that have enabled them to survive in the New World.

At the heart of the concept of "soul-force" is the African belief that the spirits of the ancestors continue among the living, giving them strength and direction. In his paean to Africa Zapata Olivella employs a veritable plethora of ancestors, seers, diviners, voodoo priests, and "gods" and their intermediaries as he moves his epic story and the characters who appear in it from Africa to America in a span of history that stretches from early times in Africa and the slave crossings to the present day. Orisha (African deities) worship requires that descendants establish a constructive relationship with the African God, with the lesser deities, and with the ancestors. *Changó, el gran putas* captures this African world view, as the novel adheres very closely to an African creed formulated recently by L. Barrett: "I believe in a supreme being who creates all things, and in lesser deities, spirits and powers who guard and control the universe. I believe in the ancestors who guard and protect their descendants. I believe in the efficacy of sacrifice and the power of magic, good and evil. And I believe in the fullness of life, here and now."[2] Nothwithstanding differences among African peoples, Barrett applies his creed to all.

The Shango Myth

The novel is structured on the myth of Shango, or on those aspects of it that can explain in African mythological terms the history of the African's enslavement and "exile" in the new land of America. Changó, or Shango, "the most popular and colorful of the orishas,"[3] is "by far the greatest hero-god of the Yoruba."[4] There are many legends about him, among them one that has him banished from his imperial kingdom, punishment for the sin of excessive pride. Versions of the legend have him unhappy with his fate and taking his own life out of disappointment and remorse. "But with all his faults he inspired and continues to inspire loyalty in his close friends. To them Shango is not dead and by continuing their loyalty to him they know they can strengthen both him and themselves."[5]

Shango, it is said, personifies masculinity with all its virtues and all its faults. This other, more positive side of the myth has this African god representing man's never-ending struggle to overcome the adversities of life. His strength, arrogance, and ability have all been translated into his followers' language of survival.[6] His own survival represents "the mythological triumph of a people . . . In the New World Shango represents the hope of a new collectivity."[7]

Both sides of the Shango myth are worked into the framework of the novel. In the first place the slave trade is explained in terms of a revenge factor: Shango, to get even with those (blacks) who turned against him and supported his banishment from the Imperial Kingdom, in turn banishes them and their descendants from their homeland, condemning them to life and "exile" in America with white people. In getting even Shango puts a "curse" on blacks. The slave trade is that curse. Secondly, after serving their penance (slavery) blacks are to welcome Shango back, and he is to infuse his descendants with his fighting spirit because it is the destiny of the African in the New World to rebel against whites and to be free. On the one hand Shango condemns blacks to a life of suffering, and on the other decrees that they, after working off the debt to him, become, like him, strong and powerful warriors who must dedicate their lives to their own liberation.

The significance of the name *Changó* in the title is that this god-protector is the guardian angel of blacks in the New World. His fighting, *macho* spirit imbues his descendants with the "soul-force" they need to overcome their oppressors. Shango and his intermediaries oversee and give direction to the black destiny in America and most of all they make certain black people never lose their will to be free. Throughout the novel characters are born and reborn with the same will or spirit passed down through generations; Zapata Olivella shows repeatedly that anyone who manifests the African spirit of resistance is really the chosen one, the spirit incarnate of Shango. Benkos, for example, for a time is "the one chosen by Shango to begin the rebellion of the African in America. Your voice will be heard in other voices, in other lives, wherever the White Wolf tramples on the shadow of a Black."[8]

The African god Changó, or Shango, then, is the key to the novel. As the author has explained, Shango is the god of fertility, dance, and war. These three attributes—*vital, danzarín,* and *guerrero*—he believes, define the black identity. The title, he is convinced, is well chosen and reflects or suggests all of these characteristics, especially the second part, which some see as pornographic: "el gran putas." Defending his title Zapata Olivella says it suggests the range of the black character that enables him to do battle with and win out both over God and the devil. What better title for the story of a people that has survived so much and for so long. Any other title, he says, would distort the meaning of the work. In a recent interview Zapata Olivella shows that he has even given some thought to the English translation of the title:

Look. I've had input from many friends during the twenty years it's taken me to put this novel together. I've discussed aspects and problems with them and especially with North American friends because there is one part of the novel—over three hundred pages—that takes place in the United States. So, in talking about these things many translations into English, especially of the Spanish title, have come up. The best one, I think, is *Shango, the Holy Fucker* (laughter). I know that the word "fucker" in English is applied without second thoughts to people for whom sex is something licentious. But if we join the word "holy" or "sacred" to it then the word "fucker" loses whatever its traditional meaning might be or it should lose it. Don't you agree? Now, I believe it's the same in both languages. The word "fucker" in the United States never carries a meaning of mediocrity; it is always used in an affirmative sense. One can use the same criteria in Spanish. Now, the word "putas" in Spanish is not only justified in the context of the work; it is also a way to take a popular expression, give it some dignity, bring it into literature and show it off to those academic writers, those masters of style who think you have to give books titles from an European tradition in accordance with Academy rules or critics who generally are no more than defenders of the system of oppression under which our people live.[9]

Myth and Structure

The novel is divided into five parts: "Los orígenes," "El Muntu americano," "La rebelión de los vodus," "Las sangres encontradas," and "Los ancestros combatientes." True to any authentic epic recounting the total black experience, Zapata Olivella's narrative starts in Africa and moves through slavery and on to racism, oppression, and economic exploitation of the black in the New World. The first chapter, "La tierra de los ancestros," appropriately is written in verse and clearly suggests the oral beginnings of black literary expression. This opening "song" is in fact an evocation of prehistory and a premonition of things to come, namely, the uprooting of Africans from the land of their ancestors. The poet calls on the spirits of the ancestors for guidance and creative skill to help him tell his story as he sings of valor, beauty, strength, and other positive qualities of the many peoples of Africa who were sent on that tragic voyage to "exile on a strange continent" (p. 16).

The poet-singer not only calls on spirits from the past for inspiration and support; he also wants the African gods and ancestors to infuse this "new American man" with this same African spirit to help him survive his martyrdom in America. The New World (America) is as much a part of this "introduction" as the Old (Africa), as there are constant references to the role of this "new man" who will enrich this new land with his blood and sweat. In the first chapter Zapata Olivella plants two ideas much repeated throughout the book, namely, that the African seed will be sown in the bloodstream of America and this new American man will also sow the seed of rebellion. These first pages, written in the mythological framework of both the curse of Shango and of his blessing, really foreshadow the entire black experience in America. Shango

passes the torch of responsibility to this new American man whose ultimate destiny is to be free. This beginning chapter, like the book itself, is
in short

a history of yesterday
forgotten histories of the future
future histories of the past
the history of the Muntu enslaved. (P. 30)

Before moving into the novel proper, then, we are introduced to African gods, kingdoms, and beliefs, and we witness the Africans' forced
separation from ancestral lands. We are also clearly presented with the
indomitable spirit of "soul-force" that will enable the African to survive
as the new man in a new world. The first test of that spirit was the slave
trade. In chapter 2, "La trata," we see various forms of black resistance
to the brutal and inhuman treatment meted out by the slave traders.
Throughout part 1 the clash of races and cultures that began with the
slave trade escalates into a war for supremacy between the religious
beliefs and practices of the two worlds. In this struggle of drum and
witchcraft against baptism and the crucifix Zapata Olivella shows the
hypocrisy of white religion and its representatives and the "magic" of
black religion and the presence of black "gods" in the lives of blacks. The
resultant incomprehension on both sides is best illustrated by the words
of one white character who, referring to blacks, wonders "if these animals have the ability to think" (p. 74), and by a black character's reference to Latin liturgical language as "obscure tongue-twisters" (p. 79)
spoken in a foreign language.

The "soul-force" of black religion sustained the African in exile and
enabled him to cope as he passed from one world to another. The differences between the two worlds were enormous, and the author presents these differences by delving into the psychological traumas created
by slavery. Slavery was a brutalizing experience for blacks, but Zapata
Olivella also presents it as a terrifying experience for the slave owners
and slave traders he depicts as unable to comprehend the Africans' perception of their situation and their gods, who never left them. The battle
between the church and its agents and the orishas and their intermedi-

aries dominates part 1. It makes for fascinating reading, and we know that the concerted effort mounted from the beginning by the African gods, the spirits of the deceased, and their heroic black descendants to take control of slave ships will continue throughout the novel and history to help blacks take control of their own fate and to become masters of the "new destiny Shango had laid out for them" (p. 91).

It is clear from the outset in part 2, "El Muntu americano," that this destiny, namely, that blacks living or dead will not rest until all blacks are free, will determine not only narrative structure but the future of the African in his "new home" as well. Part 2 opens with the difficult birth of Benkos, the chosen one for a time when the "holy war" against African religions was most heated. During this early period Africans who held on to their Africanity were treated as heretics, but Zapata Olivella shows how whites and their religion are perhaps more laden with fetishes and ritual than Africans, but without the same stigma.

The relationship developed in the novel between Benkos ("king of the Blacks," "son of Shango") and Father Claver (the "Saint of the slaves") illustrates very well the kind of relationship, according to the author, that Christianity wanted to impose on the African in the New World, namely, that he be *manso* (meek) and *sumiso* (submissive) to God and suffer in silence. To be a good servant of God, blacks are advised, they must be like a *manso animal* and not complain, advice that of course ran counter to the revolutionary mandate Benkos and his people had received from Shango. Throughout part 2 the blacks' awareness of self and their plight ran as deep as their recognition of hypocrisy in white religion: "Although the masters were having a happy holiday season we slaves knew that following the Holy Week break we would again bear the cross of slavery much heavier than the one Christ bore and for a longer time" (p. 140).

In part 2, then, we see the tremendous religious persecution launched against Africans and their beliefs, complete with the Inquisition and burnings at the stake. The New Americans objected mainly to the hypocrisy of the holy office: blacks refused to accept and worship a white God whose church kept them in chains and servitude. Zapata Olivella repeatedly makes this key point in the early section of his novel. On balance, however, he is less harsh with Father Claver, who administered to the needs of the slaves, and with Alfonso de Sandoval, whose early writings on the African in America made him, perhaps, the first Africanist scholar in America.

In part 2, and especially in part 3, "La Rebelión de los vodus," the author interprets known history in the light of the African world view. He builds this black perspective from the verse beginnings of his narrative, where he sets the stage for the intervention of the African spirit in the "destiny foreseen" of the African in America. This spirit of rebellion Africans brought to the New World leads inevitably in history and in the narrative to the Haitian Revolution, in which a high concentration of blacks sought freedom on a grand scale. Zapata Olivella presents this revolution as one more manifestation of the unstoppable movement in history toward black freedom foretold by the orishas.

The Haitian Revolution was as significant in black history as it becomes in the novel: Zapata Olivella's account of it takes up the whole of part 3, whose title, "The Voodoo Rebellion," suggests the role African beliefs had in it. The author is persistent in setting the record straight:

Our fight for freedom has been vilified with the false stigma of a racist war. When Whites oppress, murder and exploit, their cruelties are always presented in the best light and are considered civilizing acts. When the slave resists, throws off his chains and gains the upper hand his actions are considered racist, murderous and barbarous. The history of the Republic of Haiti for forgetful white historians will always be depicted as the massacre of Whites by Blacks blinded by a fanatical hatred, never as a black response to genocide perpetuated against a defenseless people. (P. 198)

African myth and ancestral beliefs are especially prevalent in Zapata Olivella's account of this revolution. He explains black persistence again as concerted effort on the part of ancestral spirits and deities acting through the corporal bodies of black people. Central to the success of this revolution, he makes clear, is the belief that "we the fallen in battle are elevated to the rank of General in the army of the deceased" (p.

180). Equally significant is the belief that ancestors and ancient deities watch over and protect black people as long as they are working for the good. And what better work than fighting for freedom?

In part 4, "Las sangres encontradas," the author continues to focus on maroon leaders like Zumbi who established the "free" territory of Palmares in Brazil, but he branches out and extends the African watch over others like Simón Bolívar in Colombia and José María Morelos in Mexico who fought for freedom and upheld the right to life and human dignity for blacks and Indians and all oppressed peoples in America. The novel has a decidedly Colombian locale in the early parts because Cartagena was a main entry port for African slaves onto the mainland. But it soon moves from Colombia to Venezuela, Haiti, Brazil, and Mexico ("land of stone head statues of African princes"), and ultimately leads to the United States in part 5.

In Part 5, "Los ancestros combatientes," Shango, through his intermediary, brings the same ancestral message of resistance to the current chosen one. By now rebellion has become a religion, "a new religion for the oppressed of all colors anywhere" (p. 349), and the blacks' survival against all odds is proof positive that Shango has singled them out for the task of liberating all people. Part 5, like the rest of the novel, is a review of black history, but presented from a black perspective. The history lesson continues into the present as many recent black heroes in the United States take their places in this narrative as part of the never-ending wave of freedom fighters moved to action by the African spirit and mandate of Shango.

Myth and Narrative Technique

From its mythological overture in verse in part 1, *Changó, el gran putas* establishes that black singers, black witnesses to history, and other black voices will tell this story. We soon learn that African deities and long-deceased ancestors exist not only to inspire and to protect; they also are often elevated to the role of narrator and like other black narrators take part in the action while telling the story from an African world view.

Few narrators are innocent bystanders: "*We* the descendants of Shango learn how to die killing" (p. 37). The reader is taken inside the ship's hold, for example, and made to share the slaves' thoughts as they plot in secret to fight back. "From below" and "from within" summarize Zapata Olivella's narrative strategies. Even when there is a narrative voice speaking from above there is always the contrasting voice from below setting the record straight. An excellent example of these contrasting views is contained in the chapter on the slave trade where the captain of the slave ship enters in his logbook his remarks about the "pieces of merchandise" in chains below. This logbook becomes another narrator and an extremely effective one because of its "outside" presentation "from above" of human suffering and events with no real understanding of them:

One of the pieces of merchandise went crazy. At first we thought it was challenging us with its shouting and spitting. The officer had it whipped to bring it under control. But crazed, it began to bite the other beasts it was chained to.

Finally we freed its feet and took it on deck and tied it to the mast. It refused to eat and just stared at us hoping we would get close enough so it could grab us or bite us. Oblivious to everything else its gaze settled on a distant point on the horizon where it seemed to bring all its thoughts to rest. I wonder if these animals have the ability to think . . . I'm trying to save it because it will bring me a good price but if it keeps on like this I'll hate to do it but I'll have to throw it to the sharks . . .

We had to throw that crazy slave overboard. It was bewitched and it laughed . . . we still heard that laughter even after it was swallowed up by the sea. (P. 78)

And later:

We have a ghost on board . . . The sailor standing watch swore he heard it following him but when he turned around to shoot it had disappeared without a trace. The following night the ship's carpenter heard someone rummaging around in his room while he was sleeping. He was paralyzed with fear . . . This ghost appeared five days after we thought we had gotten rid of that mad slave. (Pp. 75 and 79)

Zapata Olivella's contrapuntal account "from below" of what is really happening on board ship—a slave rebellion—is genuinely thrilling:

The men gathered around, some dragging pieces of the stocks they had been unable to rip from their ankles . . . The Whites hacked away at the hatch lid with their axes ready to put down the mutiny before we swarmed all over the ships. They opened up several holes but they didn't dare come down. We cut the foot off one who tried. We grabbed the foot of the most daring and cut his heel in two. The men raised their fists and their knives, the sharp points they had fashioned out of the large iron rings that had bound their hands . . . Four men helped us take the bridge; others surrounded the Captain's cabin. We know they have guns. They didn't know their time was running out . . . I saw the Captain making his last entry in his log book. The *Mandinga* woman tied to his bed saw me come in with the ax . . . and split his head open. (Pp. 88–89)

While we read from the captain's logbook how he views the slaves and their actions, we hear from the slaves themselves their plans and what motivates them. Both narrative voices are telling the same story but they are worlds apart. On the African side we have a collective narration, several narrators all telling the story from within. "I am telling you what *we* feel" (p. 140) is a poignantly intimate line that draws the reader into the world of black suffering. Black narrators present themselves as witnesses to and part of history, and this narrative role extends to the long deceased: "The deceased of Africa are not dead until the memories of them are lost to the living and even then, they are not considered totally lost," explains Leonard E. Barrett. The ancestors are not dead as long as they are remembered, especially "those whose lives were examples to their descendants."[10]

Changó, el gran putas is a fascinating display of shifting narrators who move not only from above to down below but also from this world to the next and back to guide the living. Zapata Olivella's narrative technique becomes belief incarnate. Regardless of the current narrator's identity his voice becomes a vehicle for the reappearance of ancient deities, the long deceased, and the recent dead. The ancestors exist through the lives of their descendants, and this belief brings vitality to technique as well as to character. Throughout the novel "we the dead"[11] interact with the living not in a supernatural way but to play a positive and leading role in the narrative as in the black man's destiny. What better technique to dramatize the relationship between the dead and the living in the African world view than to have the dead narrate—with a foreknowledge of the future—the story of the living.

The shifting narrator at times takes the form of sworn testimony where black voices tell much, for example, about the holy war the church declared against African religious beliefs. While these testimonies are designed to elicit damaging proof of heresy and witchcraft, the black witnesses testifying often manage to innocently cast greater negative aspersions on the customs and behavior of whites than on the "soul-force" that sustains blacks. "Rather than me," says one character, "I can tell you more about the many injustices, fornications and sodomies committed here in Cartagena by some of your leading citizens in whose hands His Majesty the King and His Holiness the Pope have entrusted the responsibility of setting good examples" (p. 123).

Historical figures take turns as narrator, always from a black perspective not often seen in historical accounts. "The French," says MacKandal, "affirm that they burned me at the stake one January 20th. They repeat this loudly and clearly on Léonarmand de Mézy's plantation where I was a slave. So there can be no doubt they spread my ashes at the Dufrené home where I was a prisoner. But my people know I will return triumphant" (p. 180). The author ends this obligatory chapter about the Haitian Revolution with yet another narrator summarizing in the form of a children's story the events of this phase of the black struggle for freedom in the New World. Even children themselves are narrators at times. In effect the novel has a collective protagonist—the black in the New World—but with many individual spokespersons as narrators. Sometimes the names change and sometimes they do not. But regardless of the narrator the destiny foretold remains the same in the end as it had been in the beginning: the inevitable freedom for Africans in exile in America. The author as storyteller never enters this novel. This abstinence or absence is especially significant because it makes way for the many eyewitnesses—both living and dead—to history who have so much to say themselves.

The main narrative feature in this novel, then, is the concept of mythical time, an "eternal now of mythical time,"[12] which allows an uninterrupted movement toward freedom where each generation of "ekobios" ("spiritual brothers" or "soul brothers") motivates later ones in a constant interaction of the living and the dead, past and present, and historical and fictional characters. The first "ekobios" were the mythological gods themselves. This technique of "mythical realism" recreates a possible reality outside chronological time where all time merges for black heroes who live their lives, pass on, and return in spirit to encourage successive generations of new heroes who inherit the mantle of leadership. The "mythical realism," or the "realm of possible realities,"[13] Zapata Olivella creates is, like "magical realism" and certainly Carpentier's "marvelous realism," a world vision that presupposes a faith, a system of belief perceived by an entire group. In his novel all of the historical characters are dead, even though they act as though they exist, and all of the living characters are inventions.

Myth, Motif, and Message

The African transplanted to America brings new blood to the New World. In slavery and in struggle blood is spilled, but there is another recurring blood motif throughout the novel. From confrontation and the clash of cultures the new American will emerge in a country enriched with the blood of the African who will not disappear in the "sea of races" (p. 32). Sexual potency associated with the reputation of Shango the womanizer is intertwined with the images of fertility, seed, sowing, and procreation, all suggesting the infusion of the African in the bloodstream of America. What started out as ethnic lynching will end in a standoff, as this mixing will take place until "there are no pure Whites left to enslave us because as we lose our color so too will Whites lose theirs" (p. 119). Only then, "when the last drop of white blood is drowned out" (p. 238), will the curse of Shango be truly lifted.

Here Zapata Olivella reverses symbols as Cubena and others had done earlier by turning white fear against itself: he attributes the negative behavior of persons of mixed blood to the "white" rather than to the "black" drop of blood. Following this line of thought this white "impure" drop makes some persons of mixed blood turn, for example, against their darker brothers. On the positive side lighter-skinned mulattoes who do side with blacks respond to the call of black consciousness and dominate the negative influence of that impure drop. Continuing the reverse symbolism, persons with that white "drop" no longer holding them back are then able to receive the guidance of the orishas and under their protection go on to great achievements.

Since part of Zapata Olivella's message is that blacks have a duty to save mankind from itself, the author seems to suggest they are a people chosen by the orishas to seek not only their own freedom but that of others on this earth as well, since it is the destiny of all men to be free. The new man in America, the "nuevo Muntu americano," like Estupiñán Bass's "nuevo Mandinga gigante," becomes a voice of hope. Both represent a new humanism and a respect for human dignity. Throughout Zapata Olivella's novel the author shows in what little regard black humanity was held. But this black experience only reinforces the need for the humanistic message blacks are destined to spread, the message that, in the final analysis, "all men are one" (p. 323).

Changó, el gran putas is an ambitious novel. The author's art and his broad aquaintance with the African pantheon enable him to show rather than to just tell the reader about the integral role the African ancestral heritage plays in the New World. By illustrating the nature of "soul-force" Zapata Olivella not only recounts the epic struggle of blacks; he also delves into the African mind and world view that made black survival possible. His account of new-world history from inside the mind of Africa and from below deck is as authentic a depiction of America's past as the slave trader's logbook. African myths, even when adapted syncretically to new-world needs, never betray ancestral memory, and the author traces the Africans' faith in their destiny from early times to today. From the slave in bondage to the positive model for liberation blacks now represent, the "saving myths that gave him [the black] a security denied to the white"[14] repeatedly played roles in black survival. The novel is saturated with a tremendous sense of commitment to this faith in one's destiny and in the power of "soul-force" to help one get there.

There is a good deal of black heroism in the novel. The instinctive individual effort we saw in *Juyungo* from Ascensión Lastre is present here in a remarkable procession of heroic black individuals. Revolutionary and rebellious zeal are constant. Black heroes in *Changó*, however, are acting out of awareness of their roles as representatives of the African collective in the New World; they know they are part of history. When they are unaware of their role, ancestral guardians not only remind them of it but help them carry it out. Ascensión Lastre, as we saw, was unaware of history and knew little of the slave trade and even less of Africa. His little awareness of the world outside Esmeraldas, however, did not inhibit Ascensión's own expression of "soul-force," which he exhibited on many occasions.

Manuel Zapata Olivella's Afro-Colombian novel is a major undertaking, but he is not the first Afro-Hispanic author to portray the role of African gods in the Afro-American revolutionary and religious tradition. Quince Duncan also used this tradition in his novel *La paz del pueblo* (1979) in which the messiah figure Pedro Dull drew inspiration and strength from ancestral spirits to resist oppression. Duncan's work in Costa Rica, like *Changó, el gran putas* in Colombia, "celebrates the important principle of vitality, of life after death, and of the interrelationship between the spirit world beyond death—the world of the 'living dead'—and the world of the living."[15] Duncan's latest published short story, "Los mitos ancestrales"[16] ("The Ancestral Myths"), like Zapata Olivella's novel *Changó, el gran putas*, uses African mythology as the basis of a fictional narrative. Carlos Guillermo Wilson's Afro-Panamanian novel *Chombo* (1981) is another recent Afro-Hispanic novel where the African belief in a spirit world beyond death comes into play. Perhaps the closest equivalent in prose by a black writer in Brazil would be the work of Deoscóredes M. dos Santos (Didi), whose short stories in the collection *Contos negros da Bahia* (1961) rely heavily on African mythology.[17]

Zapata Olivella's main objective in writing his epic, then, was not to tell the story of one character or family but of millions of blacks from

Africa dispersed throughout the New World and conceived as "one family"[18] made up of both the living and the deceased. "I wanted to write the history of the African in the New World told by Blacks themselves and not by the 'master' or slave trader."[19] In taking this approach Zapata Olivella was able to tell the story from the depths of the black African soul, in effect, to express "the souls of black folk" from an African world view. Zapata Olivella allows for the various permutations the African vision has undergone in the New World. His African world view is not that of "the pure African who preserves intact his African culture in the New World, but rather of the one whose blood and vision are mixed and enriched with that of the Indian and of Whites."[20] Thus a concession to race mixing, the only way it can be in Latin America.

The central theme in Afro-Hispanic literature and in black literature in general is liberation. In *Changó, el gran putas* Zapata Olivella goes to the source of this theme which has its roots in African "soul-force." Like Alex Haley's *Roots* the Afro-Colombian's novel also returns to the past to help explain the present. The inspiration is African, but the Shango saga is, in the end, a saga of America.

Chapter Seven

I would . . . keep alive in our hearts
a sense of the inexpressible human.

—Richard Wright

Toward
a Human
Poetics

A Role for Black Literature

Black writers in Latin America will continue to gain much-needed visibility as their works are increasingly studied, more widely incorporated in the humanities curriculum, and translated into other languages. This development is significant because of the humanistic role black literature plays in the search for *la especifidad latinoamericana*. Black literature opens windows to Latin American literature, but through a perspective seen "from below" and "from within." This perspective is important and balances very well the better-known views "from above." It has been said that the history of America "looks very different from a cotton patch."[1] Something similar can be paraphrased for Latin America, whose history indeed looks very different from below a slave ship deck.

Black literature has a role to play not just in Latin American history but in the classroom as well because it provides models for both black and nonblack students seeking humanistic statements about life. Black literature relates in Latin America, as elsewhere, to the struggle for human dignity, and it teaches readers how to live and how to seek the freedom that should be an automatic quality of one's life. The theme of liberty, so prominently displayed in Zapata Olivella's *Changó, el gran putas*, is an outstanding one in black literature, but it is in the real lives of black people that this theme takes root. Blacks must see this literature's relevance to their own feelings about racial, social, political, and humanistic questions. This is really what black literature teaches: knowing oneself through one's own models and examples, both in literature and in the real life literature reflects.

In our classrooms we should focus on black role models in literature and in our background reading to literature. We should emphasize, for example, that blacks' passion for liberty and what has been called their "stubbornness"[2] in fighting for it probably influenced Latin American whites and *mestizos* in their own secession and independence struggles. We should emphasize that black Latin Americans who accommodated themselves to their status as slaves or as second-class citizens following abolition were rare and that, as we saw repeatedly in *Changó, el gran putas*,

[t]he most fierce, refractory, or impatient, and those who were most mistreated or neglected by white culture, said "no" to acculturation and assimilation, and preferred to run away from the plantations and to isolate themselves individually or collectively, in Latin America's *selvas*, bush, mountains, and other open spaces. They were the *cimarrones* of Spanish America, the *maroons* of British America, *les marrons* of French America, and those who formed their *quilombos* in Portuguese America.[3]

Large-scale black revolts occurred everywhere in Latin America. The two most well known were the black rebellion in Brazil in 1627, when deserting slaves founded their independent and well-organized Republic of Palmares and held it for seventy years,[4] and the slave uprisings in Haiti in 1793 which culminated in the country's independence in 1804. The black's passion for liberty has pervaded Latin America. Black people have been not only a valuable element in Latin America's nation-founding process[5] but the major architect of their own liberation as well. It is not surprising, therefore, that the theme of liberty is a major one in black literature in the Americas.

The quest for freedom, especially when paired with the search for identity, is a strong motivating factor. But there is another quest, the quest for literacy, which again points to the example black writers provide for the classroom student looking for models to emulate. It has been said that "the great gift of the best Afro-American literature to its readers is its historical and linguistic portrait of a culture . . . questing for, finding, and relishing the written word."[6] This quest for literacy by a "people once imprisoned by an enforced illiteracy"[7] has produced many self-made men and women from the days of slavery to our times who have left remarkable testimonies of this relish for the written word, and for the spoken word too, as oral performance often found its way into the formal literature of technically accomplished writers in the Americas. The novels of the Afro–Costa Rican author Quince Duncan and the experimental literature of Nelson Estupiñán Bass in Ecuador and Cuba's Nicolás Guillén, for example, exemplify this relish, as does the erudition displayed by Panama's Carlos Guillermo Wilson and Colombia's Manuel Zapata Olivella, among others.

Correctness of Vision

In our rush, however, to acclaim the technical accomplishments of black writers we must not lose sight of the rehumanizing role black literature has brought to bear on the concept of literary Americanism; nor should we ignore the comeback humanistic criticism in general is making when we analyze black literature. Humanistic criticism has fast established itself as one of the leading critical approaches to literature today. The concept, which embodies a return to the human, reemerged generally as a reaction against the dehumanization of art (to use the descriptive phrase introduced by José Ortega y Gasset years ago) that has characterized literary theory and the critical analysis of literary texts for the greater part of this century. More specifically, humanistic criticism reemerged as a challenge to the scientific methodologies of the formalists, the New Critics, and the structuralists.

    Humanistic criticism, quite simply put, "sees man at the centre as the creator of forms"[8] and the literary work as something "made by somebody"[9] in response to lived experience. Humanistic criticism has become one of the dominant poststructuralist activities because, in effect, it rejects the autonomous or the autotelic theory of literature and sees interaction between *text* and *context,* or between literature and its cultural, racial, and historical circumstances. To the humanist critic literature "is relevant to matters outside of it or it is nothing, however internally unified."[10] Unlike a more scientific approach, humanistic criticism does not view the literary work as a self-contained creation existing in its own right, detached from author and from society. Rather than seeing literature as remote "from life itself . . . inhuman and unliving,"[11] the humanist critic believes that preoccupation with the moral and human content of literature is not incompatible with aesthetic enjoyment.

Addison Gayle, Jr., like Miguel Angel Asturias before him, contributed to the development of a human poetics when he rejected critical methodology as irrelevant—certainly to the black community—if it does not aid men in becoming better than they are. This well-known aesthetician asserted quite firmly that "the question for the black critic today is not how beautiful is a melody, a play, a poem or a novel, but how much more beautiful has the poem, melody, play or novel made the life of a single black man."[12] What Gayle rejects, in effect, is a criticism that evokes only "the emptiness of a game, not the richness of human possibility."[13] I take this quote from Eugene Goodheart's recent book *The Failure of Criticism,* whose suggestive title forecasts his main themes, namely, the disappearance of the moral sense in contemporary avant-garde criticism and the loss of authority humanistic criticism has suffered in this century. Equally concerned that humanistic criticism, or a criticism which has as its object the quality of life, has lost ground, the late John Gardner also was vehement in his rejection of game-oriented criticism, and he extended Goodheart's argument by focusing on the moral quality of fiction in his book *On Moral Fiction.*[14]

What Gardner advocated, it seems, was the "old-fashioned" or "traditional" view of what art is and does, and what, according to Gardner the fundamental business of critics ought to be. His traditional view, which echoes Gayle's controversial position, is that true art is moral since it seeks to improve life, not debase it. Gardner believed that New Critics, structuralists, formalists, linguistic philosophers, and other "aesthetic game players" (as he called them) who tell us that works of art are like trees—simply objects for perception—all avoid on principle such humanistic questions as whom will this work of art help.

Like Gardner, John Reichert argues for a moral—as opposed to a purely formal or literary—evaluation of literature. In chapter 3, "Writer and Reader," of his recent book *Making Sense of Literature*,[15] Reichert recognizes the importance of the author's intent and the reader's response in literary interpretation. In "Evaluation,"[16] his final chapter, he insists that there are ways of describing literary values from an evaluative, and sometimes moral, point of view. Reichert believes literature should relate to human experiences, concerns, and choices. Moral assumptions can be made, he insists, provided the critical essay is not turned into a treatise on morality and social ethics. The moral quality in a work enriches our lives and "makes us better." Literature gives insight to and throws light on human issues, human freedom, and on "the rich experience of 'humans living.' "[17] Humanistic criticism seeks this insight by focusing on the human in literature partly as a reaction against a science of literature and partly in continuation of the old moral purpose the humanistic tradition is noted for.

Humanistic critics do not suggest that the study of literature be replaced with the study of its readers, the society in which the work is created, or with the author; they do recognize, however, that sociological criticism, which resists the linguistic world view of structuralism, comes closest to the kind of criticism they advocate. Aware that literature is a social product, they recognize that literary sociology does indeed have the potential "for bringing literary study back into the service of human needs."[18] Recognizing literature to be a product of human beings in their relations with others, they argue that literary sociology can help criticism "retain its claim to being a humanistic discipline."[19]

Humanistic criticism, in short, looks to literature for what we as readers find significant or relevant to life. Northrop Frye, I believe, once said that when a critic interprets, he is talking about his poet; and when he evaluates, he is talking about himself. This subjective reaction to the literary work as it relates to our lives and to what a reader feels rather than to how a work fits into the pattern of a preimposed method is of interest to the humanistic critic. Not only, then, does the author write out of experience, but the critic as well evaluates out of experience. Finding human relevance, or seeing literature as relevant to the human experience of both author and reader, is a crucial task of humanistic criticism. Humanistic criticism builds on the premise that art is primarily what John Gardner called "correctness of vision."[20] Tracing this vision from the generating idea through to its technical, concrete manifestation is the task of the humanist critic, especially if we are to bring a moral judgment to bear on the author's work, and on its relevance to ethnic, social, and human values.

Humanism in the Classroom

Humanistic criticism is making a comeback not just in Latin America but elsewhere as well, which is why the heavy stress on formalistic "textuality" and "intertextuality" is unexpected in *Afro-American Literature: The Reconstruction of Instruction,* edited by Dexter Fisher and Robert Stepto. This recent publication rightly responds to the need for new course designs and critical approaches to Afro-American literature, but in light of recent movement toward humanistic criticism it seems surprising that this valuable work does not stress it. Dexter Fisher writes that "until we perceive Afro-American literature as an act of language, we will have missed its complexity and gleaned only a fraction of what it contributes to the larger arena of humanistic endeavors."[21] But Fisher then makes the ultimate antihumanistic statement: "An effective course, for example, will focus on the way certain literary texts relate linguistically to one another rather than on how they fit into a chronological scheme."[22] This intertextual approach requires close reading on individual texts, but the danger here is that too close attention to the transition between texts can discourage the search for the broader relationship between literary chronology or literary history and the black experiences which that literature reflects. Literature is a "linguistic event," but it is certainly more than that.

The intent of *Afro-American Literature: The Reconstruction of Instruction* is laudable and has to be respected as a literary approach to black literature, but do we still need to prove that black literature can withstand such scrutiny? One author insists that refusal to use sophisticated analysis on black literature smacks of a symbolic inferiority complex as blatant as were treatments of skin lightener and hair straightener. But this felt need to subject black literature to "close reading" to prove that it is not inferior reveals in itself a measure of insecurity. Besides, sophisticated analysis sometimes loses sight of the obvious. For example, it is not *Juyungo*'s "affair with the sign"[23] that makes Ortiz's novel memorable, nor do we have to refer to the slave narratives as a "system of signs"[24] to know what slave writings were all about.

The correctness of vision embodied in a humanistic approach has to extend beyond charting resonances among black literary works. In the classroom, one has to seek the human element in black literature and look not only at literature by blacks but also at creative literature on black themes, at critical literature, and at the teacher's role. Just as important as teaching black literature is the need to guard against the distortion of the black person's humanity which racist literary images often propagate in the classroom. Humanism is as much what teachers and students bring into the classroom as what they get out of the works under discussion. Humanism is what the creative artists put into their works, but just as important is the human reading we bring to these works and to the criticism of them. This reading is especially important in the classroom, where students have to be taught not only to look for linguistic patterns and intertextual links but also to reevaluate literature in human terms, particularly when that literature has some relevance to their own lives. No black reader, for example, can read literature about the black experience dispassionately, especially if that literature is written by a white racist. Humanistic criticism of a text seeks out the human in it and endeavors to see how it is expressed thematically through language. The text is an act of language, a linguistic event, but put to what purpose and with what results?

These questions have to be explored because there is an upswing of courses and publications on blacks in Latin American literature, and some guidelines are necessary. Overriding guidelines, however, is the humanism one should look for in the text, in the author, in the critic, in the teacher, and in oneself. Humanism must be in the critic and the teacher before it can be found in literature (the text, the author) and passed on to the reader (the student). Credibility is especially important in the teacher because teaching black literature and literature on black themes involves more than teaching what is literary about that literature. In a literature course the focal point should be the literature in question, but aspects of literary creation can hardly be of interest when there is a credibility gap between the racially aware student and the creative and critical literature he is studying and the teacher who is teaching it. A humanistic attitude on the part of the teacher can help bridge a credibility gap, should one exist. Color does matter in the creative writer, the critic, the teacher, and the reader if it becomes an obstacle to the propagation of the credible black image.

Black literature represents humanism in action, and the humanistic goal of literary criticism should be, in part, to motivate blacks and others to search for the credible black image and the true black experience while affirming the humanity of black people everywhere. Black Studies in general has been called "an invitation to communion"[25] and to begin again. Much of the new work in the field of Afro-Hispanic literature represents a new beginning. Black Studies, Julius Lester has said, "begins with the lives of black people and reaches out to all humanity."[26] This is especially true in Latin America where the literature of Afro–Latin American authors represents a human poetics.

The Black Legacy

Julius Lester has made more sense than most in his article on Black Studies, particularly his insistence that Black Studies represents a different point of view, one rooted in the ethnic memory of past experience. Black Studies in general, according to Lester, "grows down"[27] to incorporate the perspective of those who live that experience. I like what Lester has to say on this point because it underscores the reversal of symbols taking place in Latin America and the recognition of the role model black literature plays in that part of the world. By "growing down" Latin American literature can see in the black legacy an authentic reflection of the humanistic premise that has become a *constante* in that literature and in the concept of literary Americanism that defines it.

When Lester writes that understanding the "freedom" Bigger (in *Native Son*) felt after an act of murder is more important than talking about Richard Wright's technique as a novelist, we know that he has come very close to understanding what Emile Snyder[28] meant when he chose to gamble first on what appears most human in literature, asking only later for the substantiation of literary aesthetics. "The mission of Black Studies," Lester has written, "is to invite and guide students into human experience."[29] The same can be said specifically for black literature in Latin America because it brings a humanistic message into the classroom and into our institutions of higher learning. This message is simply Jesse Jackson's "I am somebody" translated into positive academic action and image-building crystallized in the expression "I matter as a human being."

This message is the essence of the black legacy that has infused Latin American life and literature from the time of slavery to the present day with the quality of being human. Black humanist values are part of the African continuum in America, and black writers for years have been injecting these values into Latin American literature from below and from within. The black presence has been a positive presence, and to read black literature is to understand what it means to survive the inhumanities of this earth. The fact that blacks resisted dehumanization and survived slavery makes meaningful much of what they say not only about their own black experiences but also about the American experience in general, which has benefited from the black example. Black voices in Latin America, by affirming black humanity, become models of what true American voices should be.

The humanist value of the black legacy, namely, protest against human slavery of any kind and respect for the rights and dignity of the human being, is not exclusively African. There have been others from other cultures and traditions in Europe and the New World who have spoken, often self-critically, against what has been called "the underdeveloped heart."[30] The Africanist movement in the early part of this century, when white writers, largely in Europe and America, attacked negative aspects of Western civilization, is a case in point. But even as they undermined the so-called intellectual superiority of the white world, something of value was found in the black sensibility that expressed not only that sensibility but the deepest longings of humanity in general.

What we got out of the Africanist movement was that the heritage of blackness was more humanizing when compared to the dehumanizing influence of a mechanistic and technological Western civilization known for its history of slavery, racism, and racial discrimination. Part of the black legacy in Latin America comes wrapped in images of song, dance, rhythm, and oral expression, but it is in the deeper ethos or set of humanist values that a lasting legacy took root. This legacy can be traced from the *Afrocriollo* movement which provided firm roots for literary Americanism in the 1920s and the 1930s, and from the racial *contextos* of magic realism and the marvelous reality of the new-world black observed in the 1940s and 1950s, to the Caliban or Third World symbol in the 1960s and 1970s and from there to the Afro model black writers provide in the 1980s. Whatever the historical or literary moment, the humanist values of blacks have helped give balance to Latin America's larger society of which they form a part.

There is more to the black legacy in Latin America than cultural influences; more even than the black's energy, "spirituality, emotional warmth, vitality and intuitiveness."[31] There is also more than the sense of decolonialization Nicolás Guillén's *son* poems, for example, represent in terms of dependency, and there is even more to that legacy than the Shango mandate: the black's infectious love of freedom. The black legacy is found in all of these contributions but it is their sum total value, or the overall humanizing impact of the black as an enduring human presence and theme, that gives a corrective balance to Latin American literature. Black humanism derives from blacks' discovery of their own humanity as well as from the realization that they have become, over the years, not only defenders and representatives of nations and symbols or preservers of national cultures but also symbolic guardians of humanity in general. Perhaps in the final analysis Africa's greatest gift to the West has been her moral and humanist values which continue to guide the poetics of the black writer in Latin America.

Notes

Introduction

1. See J. B. Kubayanda, "Hispanic Humanism and Nineteenth-Century Cuban Blacks: An Historico-Literary Perspective," *Plantation Society* 1, no. 3 (1981): 343–63.
2. Michael Benamou, "The Concept of Marginality in Ethnopoetics," in *Minority Language and Literature,* ed. Dexter Fisher (New York: Modern Language Association, 1977), 151.
3. J. B. Kubayanda, "Afrocentric Hermeneutics and the Rhetoric of *transculturación* in Black Latin American Literature." In *Latin America and the Caribbean: Geopolitics, Development, and Culture* (Ottawa: CALACS, 1983), 226–40.
4. Jerome Rothenberg, "Preface to a Symposium on Ethnopoetics," in *Alcheringa,* ed. Michel Benamou and Jerome Rothenberg (Boston: Boston University Press, 1976), 7.
5. Ibid., 6.
6. Ibid.
7. E. Bradford Burns, "Bartholomé Mitre: The Historian As Novelist, the Novel As History," *Revista interamericana de bibliografía* 32, no. 2 (1982): 160.
8. Rothenberg, "Symposium on Ethnopoetics," 7.
9. Ibid., 8.
10. David Antin, "Talking to Discover," in *Alcheringa,* 112.
11. Sylvia Wynter, "Ethno or Socio Poetics," *Alcheringa,* 78–94.
12. Jean Franco, *The Modern Culture of Latin America: Society and the Artist* (Middlesex, England: Penguin Books, 1970), 55.
13. Eugene Perkins, "The Changing Status of Black Writers," *Black World* (June 1970): 95.
14. David Brookshaw, *Race and Color in Brazilian Literature* (Metuchen, N.J.: Scarecrow Press, 1986).

One. The Authenticity Question

1. Fernando Ainsa, "La espiral abierta de la novela latinoamericana (notas para la construcción de un sistema novelesco)," in *Novelas hispanoamericanas de hoy,* ed. Juan Loveluck (Madrid: Taurus, 1976), 23.
2. Augusto Roa Bastos, "Imagen y perspectivas de la narrativa latinoamericana," *Novelas hispanoamericanas de hoy,* 49.
3. Pedro Grases, "De la novela en América," *Mesa rodante* 1 (1949): 9–17. Reprinted in *La novela hispanoamericana,* 2d ed., ed. Juan Loveluck (Santiago: Editorial Universitaria, 1966), 97–105.
4. José Antonio Portuondo, "El rasgo predominante en la novela hispanoamericana," in *La novela iberoamericana,* Proceedings of the Fifth International Congress of Iberoamerican Literature (Albuquerque: University of New Mexico Press, 1951), 77–87. Reprinted in Loveluck, *La novela hispanoamericana,* 121–29.
5. In Luis Harss and Barbara Dohman, *Into the Mainstream: Conversations with Latin American Writers* (New York: Harper and Row, 1967), 91–92.
6. Ibid., 91.
7. See Gustav Segade, "Central Issues in Contemporary Latin American Poetic Theory" (Ph.D. diss., University of Arizona, 1972).
8. Federico de Onís, "Rubén Darío, 1867–1916," *La torre,* año 15, nos. 55 and 56 (Jan.–June 1967): 23.
9. Rubén Darío, *Poesías completas* (Madrid: Aguilar, 1961), 546.
10. Cited in de Onís, "Rubén Darío," 23.
11. See Richard L. Jackson, *The Black Image in Latin American Literature* (Albuquerque: University of New Mexico Press, 1976), 76–77.
12. José Enrique Rodó, *Obras completas,* ed. Emir Rodríquez Monegal (Madrid: Aguilar, 1967), 869.
13. Ibid., 869.
14. Keith Ellis, *Critical Approaches to Rubén Darío* (Toronto: University of Toronto Press, 1974), 100.
15. César Vallejo, "Parado en una piedra," *Obra poética completa* (Lima: Francisco Moncloa Editores, 1968), 335.
16. Jean Franco, *César Vallejo: The Dialectics of Poetry and Silence* (Cambridge: Cambridge University Press, 1976), 148.
17. See, for example, José Carlos Mariátegui, *Seven Interpretative Essays on Peruvian Reality,* trans. Majory Urquidi (Austin: University of Texas Press,

1971), 252, and Américo Ferrari, "Prólogo," in Vallejo, *Obra poética completa,* 17.

18. Pablo Neruda, "Discurso al Congreso de la Paz," vol. 2, *Poesía política de Pablo Neruda* (Santiago de Chile: Editorial Austral, 1953), 224.

19. Ibid., 222.

20. Pablo Neruda, *Obras completas* (Buenos Aires: Losada, 1967), 347.

21. Pablo Neruda, *Fin de mundo* (Buenos Aires: Losada, 1969), 180.

22. Nicolás Guillén, *Obra poética, 1920–1972,* vol. 1 (Havana: Editorial de Arte y Literatura, 1974), 120.

23. Neruda, *Obras completas,* 242.

24. José Ortega, "Pablo Neruda: The Making of a Political Poet," in *Perspectives on Contemporary Literature,* ed. Bonnie Reynolds (Louisville: University of Louisville Press, 1976), 4.

25. Ortega, "Pablo Neruda," 4.

26. George Yudice, "The Poetics of Breakdown," *Review* 23 (1978): 20.

27. In Bruce Novoa, introduction to "History According to Pao Cheng," *Latin American Literary Review* 6, no. 12 (1978): 122.

28. Mario Benedetti, "El escritor y la crítica en el contexto del subdesarrollo," *Casa de las Américas,* no. 107 (1978): 7.

29. Ibid., 7.

30. Arturo Torres Rioseco, *Grandes novelistas de la América Hispana,* (Berkeley: University of California Press, 1941).

31. Luis Alberto Sánchez, *Proceso y contenido de la novela hispanoamericana,* 2d ed. (Madrid: Editorial Gredos, 1968).

32. Fernando Alegría, *Historia de la novela hispanoamericana,* 3d ed. (Mexico: Ediciones de Andrea, 1966).

33. Zunilda Gertel, *La novela hispanoamericana contemporánea* (Buenos Aires: Editorial Colomba, 1971).

34. Cedomil, Goic, *Historia de la novela hispanoamericana* (Valparaíso: Ediciones Universitarias de Valparaíso, 1972).

35. Mario Vargas Llosa, "La novela primitiva y la novela de creación en América Latina," *Revista de la Universidad de México* 23, no. 10 (1969): 29–33.

36. Ramón Xirau, "Crisis del realismo," in *América Latina en su literatura,* ed. César Fernández Moreno (Mexico: Siglo Veintiuno Editores, 1972), 185–203.

37. Jorge Enrique Adoum, "El realismo de la otra realidad," in *América Latina en su literatura,* 204–18.

38. See José Luis Martín, *La narrativa de Vargas Llosa, Acercamiento estilístico* (Madrid: Editorial Gredos, 1974) for examples of revolutionary and experimental techniques used by Cortázar, Sarduy, Elizondo, and others.

39. "The problem is that we are not European . . . we are Latin American and certain phenomena typically European like the *nouveau roman* or even the *nouvelle critique* seem to us to be a big waste of talent." Mario Benedetti, "Situación del intelectual en la América Latina," *Diez años de la Revista Casa de las Américas, 1960–1970* 6 (1970): 152–53.

40. William L. Siemens, "Guillermo Cabrera Infante's *Tres tristes tigres,*" in *Graduate Studies on Latin America: The University of Kansas,* ed. Charles L. Stansifer (Lawrence: University of Kansas, 1973), 75.

41. Andrés Amorós, *Introducción a la novela hispanoamericana actual* (Salamanca: Ediciones Anaya, 1971), 22.

42. Manuel Pedro González, "La novela hispanoamericana en el contexto de lo internacional," in *Coloquio sobre la novela hispanoamericana,* ed. Ivan A. Schulman et al. (Mexico: Tezontle, 1967), 43.

43. Ibid., 37–112.

44. Ibid., 42.

45. Oscar Collazos et al., *Literatura en la revolución y revolución en la literatura* (Mexico: Siglo Veintiuno Editores, 1970).

46. Robert G. Mead, Jr., "After the Boom," *Américas* 30 (1978): 2–8.

47. Hernán Vidal, *Literatura hispanoamericana e ideología liberal: Surgimiento y crisis* (Buenos Aires: Hispamérica, 1976), 102.

48. Ibid., 102.

49. Jean Franco, "The Crisis of the Liberal Imagination," *Ideologies and Literature* 1 (December 1976–January 1977): 5–24.

50. Ibid., 21–22.

51. Ibid., 22.

52. Marta Sánchez, "Caliban: The New Latin American Protagonist of *The Tempest,*" *Diacritics* 6 (1976): 54–61. Also see her "Three Latin American Novelists in Search of *lo Americano*: A Productive Failure" (Ph.D. diss., University of California, San Diego, 1977).

53. Carlos Blanco Aguinaga, "Sobre la idea de la novela en Carlos Fuentes," chapter 4 in *De mitólogos y novelistas* (Madrid: Ediciones Turner, 1975), 73–108.

54. Marta Sánchez, "Caliban," 57.

55. Mario Vargas Llosa, "Social Commitment and the Latin American Writer," *World Literature Today* 58 (1978): 5–14.

56. Ibid., 14.

57. Ibid., 13.

58. In Ronald Christ, "Talk with Vargas Llosa," *New York Times Book Review,* April 9, 1978, 33.

59. José Miguel Oviedo, cited in Jorge Ruffinelli, "La crítica literaria, hoy," *Texto crítico* 6 (1977): 25.

60. Domingo Miliani, cited in Ruffinelli, "La crítica literaria," 25.

61. William Katra, "Cultural Dependency and Literature in Latin America," *Buckham Literary Studies: Michigan State University* 6 (1975): 4.

62. Ibid., 7.

63. António Cândido, "Literatura y subdesarrollo," in *América Latina en su literatura,* ed. César Fernández Moreno (Mexico: Siglo Veintiuno Editores, 1972), 351.

64. Mario Benedetti, "Temas y Problemas," in *América Latina en su literatura,* 367.

65. Angel Rama, *Diez problemas para el novelista latinoamericano* (Caracas: Síntesis Dosmil, 1972), 9.

66. Mead, "After the Boom," 3.

67. Ibid., 5.

68. Sánchez, "Three Latin American Novelists in Search of *Lo Americano,* xv.

69. Juan Loveluck, *Novelistas hispanoamericanos de hoy,* 16.

70. Segade, "Central Issues in Contemporary Latin American Poetic Theory."

71. Antonio Cornejo Polar, "El indigenismo y las literaturas heterogéneas: Su doble estatuto socio-cultural," *Revista de crítica literaria,* año 4, nos. 7–8 (1978): 7–21.

72. Ibid., 7.

Two. From Black Folk Up

1. Robert González Echevarría, *Alejo Carpentier: The Pilgrim at Home* (Ithaca: Cornell University Press, 1978), 42.

2. Lloyd King, "Nicolás Guillén and *Afrocubanismo,*" in *A Celebration of Black and African Writings,* ed. Bruce King and Kolawole Ogung-Besan. (Zaria and Ibadan, Nigeria: Ahmadu Bello University Press, 1975), 32.

3. González Echevarría, *The Pilgrim at Home,* 4.

4. Ibid., 5.

5. King, "Nicolás Guillén," 33.

6. Frank Janney, *Alejo Carpentier and His Early Works* (London: Tamesis Books, 1981), 14.

7. Juan Antonio Corretjer, *El Mundo* (San Juan), 1938, reprinted in G. R. Coulthard, *Race and Colour in Caribbean Literature* (London: Oxford University Press, 1962), 54.

8. Lemuel Johnson, " 'El tema negro': The Nature of Primitivism in the Poetry of Luis Palés Matos," in *Blacks in Hispanic Literature: Critical Essays,* ed. Miriam DeCosta (Port Washington, N.Y.: Kennikat Press, 1977), 127.

9. See Coulthard, *Race and Colour,* 30–31.

10. Janney, *Alejo Carpentier,* 19.

11. González Echevarría, *The Pilgrim at Home,* 46.

12. Ibid., 47.

13. Feme Ojo-Ade, "De origen africano, soy cubano: African Elements in the Literature of Cuba," *African Literature Today,* no. 9 (1978): 54.

14. Efraín Barradas, "Cigarro, Colón: Ciclón: Ciclo: nota para una relectura de *Ecué Yambá O,*" *Sin nombre* 12, no. 2 (1981): 81–95.

15. Janney, *Alejo Carpentier,* 24.

16. Ibid., 35.

17. Ibid., 20.

18. René Dépestre, "Problems of Identity for the Black Man in Caribbean Literature," *Caribbean Quarterly* 19 (1973): 55.

19. Ibid., 56.

20. In Angel Augier, *Nicolás Guillén:, Notas para un estudio biográfico-crítico,* vol. 1 (Havana: Universidad Central de las Villas, 1962), 99. Reprinted in Ojo-Ade, "De origen africano," 52.

21. Ojo-Ade, "De origen africano," 54.

22. *Motivos de son,* reprinted in Guillén's *Obra poética, 1920–1972,* vol. 1 (Havana: Editorial de Arte y Literatura, 1974), 101–10.

23. Nicolás Guillén, *Prosa de prisa, 1929–1972,* vol. 1 (Havana: Editorial Arte y Literatura, 1975), 5.

24. Ibid., 100.

25. In Nancy Morejón, "Conversación con Nicolás Guillén," *Recopilación de textos sobre Nicolás Guillén* (Havana: Casa de las Américas, 1974), 42.

26. Augier, *Nicolás Guillén* 1:115.

27. Mirta Aguirre, "El cincuentenario de *Motivos de son,*" in Nicolás Guillén, *Motivos de son* (Havana: Editorial Letras Cubanas, 1980), 5.

28. Ian Smart, "Nicolás Guillén's *son* Poem: An African Contribution to Con-

temporary Caribbean Poetics," *College Language Association Journal* 23 (1980): 362.

29. Aguirre, "El cincuentenario de *Motivos de son*," 9.

30. Lorna Williams, *Self and Society in the Poetry of Nicolás Guillén* (Baltimore: Johns Hopkins University Press, 1982).

31. Martha K. Cobb, *Harlem, Haiti, and Havana: A Comparative Study of Langston Hughes, Jacques Roumain, and Nicolás Guillén* (Washington, D.C.: Three Continents Press, 1979), 106.

32. See Guillén, *Prosa de prisa, 1929–1972*, vol. 1.

33. Stephanie Davis-Lett, "Blacks and *Criollismo:* A Curious Relationship," *College Language Association Journal* 24, no. 2 (1980): 131–49.

34. Kessel Schwartz, *A New History of Spanish-American Fiction*, vol. 1 (Coral Gables: University of Miami Press, 1972), 147.

35. Davis-Lett, "Blacks and *Criollismo,* 142.

36. Ibid., 149.

37. González Echevarría, *The Pilgrim at Home*, 49.

38. Ibid.

39. Ibid., 43.

40. Ibid., 126.

41. Ibid., 123.

42. Ray Verzasconi, "Magical Realism and the Literary World of Miguel Angel Asturias," (Ph.D. diss., University of Washington, 1965), 17 and 244.

43. James Irish, "Magic Realism: A Search for Caribbean and Latin American Roots," *Literary Half Yearly* 2 (1971): 127–39.

44. Ibid., 130.

45. Ibid., 131.

46. Ibid., 133.

47. Ibid., 136.

48. Roberto Fernández Retamar, *Calibán: Apuntes sobre la cultura en nuestra América* (Mexico: Editorial Diógenes, 1921). First published in *Casa de las Américas*, año 12, no. 68 (1971), this work has been translated into English by Lynn Garafola et al. as "Caliban: Notes Toward a Discussion of Culture in Our America," *The Massachusetts Review* 15 (1974): 7–72.

49. Magnus Mörner, *Race Mixture in the History of Latin America* (Boston: Little, Brown and Co., 1967), 149.

50. For more on Nascimento's view of "the real Brazil" see Doris J. Turner's "Symbols in Two Afro-Brazilian Literary Works: *Jubiabá* and *Sortilégio*," in

Teaching Latin American Studies, ed. Miriam Williford and J. Doyle Castell (Gainesville, Fla.: Latin American Studies Association, 1977), 41–58.

Three. Modern Black Heroism

1. See Annette Ivory Dunzo, "Black Heroes in the Theatre of Early Spain," in *Homenaje a Lydia Cabrera,* ed. Reinaldo Sánchez et al. (Miami: Ediciones Universal, 1978), 267–74, and her "Blacks of Sub-Saharan African Origin in Spain: Image in the Theatre, 1500–1700" (Ph.D. diss., U.C.L.A., 1974).
2. Martha Cobb, "Afro-Arabs, Blackamoors, and Blacks: An Inquiry into Race Concepts through Spanish Literature," in *Blacks in Hispanic Literature,* ed. Miriam DeCosta (Port Washington, N.Y.: Kennikat Press, 1977), 26.
3. Dunzo, "Black Heroes," 272.
4. Ibid., 270.
5. Dunzo, "Blacks of Sub-Saharan African Origin," 193.
6. Jonathan Tittler, "*Juyungo*/Reading Writing," in *Voices from Under: Black Narrative in Latin America and the Caribbean,* ed. William Luis (Westport, Conn.: Greenwood Press, 1984), 167.
7. Shirley Anne Williams, *Give Birth to Brightness* (New York: Dial Press, 1972), 58.
8. Ibid., 215.
9. Richard Jackson, *Black Writers in Latin America* (Albuquerque: University of New Mexico Press, 1979), 122.
10. Adalberto Ortiz, *Juyungo,* trans. Susan Hill and Jonathan Tittler (Washington: Three Continents Press, 1982), 20. References carried in the text are to this edition.
11. Adalberto Ortiz, *Juyungo* (Barcelona: Seix Barral, 1976), 58.
12. Ortiz, *Juyungo,* trans. Hill and Tittler, 70.
13. Jonathan Tittler, *Voices from Under,* 14.
14. Adalberto Ortiz, *Juyungo,* trans. Hill and Tittler, 195.
15. Antonio Olliz Boyd, "The Concept of Black Esthetics As Seen in Selected Works of Three Latin American Writers: Machado de Assis, Nicolás Guillén, and Adalberto Ortiz" (Ph.D. diss., Stanford University, 1975), 203.
16. Martha Cobb, "Ortiz, Glissant, and Ellison: Fictional Patterns in Black Literature," *Afro-Hispanic Review* 1, no. 3 (1982): 6.
17. Ibid., 6.

18. Ronna Newman, "Life and Works of Adalberto Ortiz," (Ph.D. diss., North-western University, 1981).

19. Ibid., 92.

20. Carl Jung, quoted in Newman, "Life and Works," 93.

21. Ortiz, *Juyungo,* trans. Hill and Tittler, 143.

22. Tittler, *Voices from Under,* 17 and 20.

23. Marisol Ballester, "Three Possibilities for Black Liberation in *Juyungo,*" *Afro-Hispanic Review* 2, no. 2 (1983): 5–6.

24. Anne Cauley, "A Definition of Freedom in the Fiction of Richard Wright," *College Language Association Journal* 19, no. 3 (1976): 332.

25. Ibid.

26. Ibid., 334.

27. Newman, "Life and Works," 181.

28. Carol Beane, "The Characterization of Blacks and Mulattoes in Selected Novels from Colombia, Venezuela, Ecuador, and Peru" (Ph.D. diss., University of California, Berkeley, 1980), 154.

29. Tittler, *Voices from Under,* 9.

30. Ibid., 16.

31. Examples of the black as hero in the Caribbean and in Brazil are discussed in two recent essays both appearing in *Voices from Under:* Juris Sileniek ("The Maroon Figure in Caribbean Francophone Prose"), and Ronald M. Rassner ("Palmares and the Freed Slave in Afro-Brazilian Literature"). Both authors highlight the literary image of the black as a heroic rebel against injustice in the respective areas, as I have done here in the case of Juyungo in Esmeraldas.

Four. The Great New **Mandinga**

1. See Emir Rodríquez Monegal, "The Metamorphoses of Caliban," *Diacritics* 7 (1977): 78–83.

2. Ian Smart, "Some Thoughts on the African Contribution to Spanish Literature," *Ufahamu* 7 (1977): 85.

3. Smart, "African Contribution to Spanish Literature," 86.

4. See Jean Franco, "Criticism and Literature within the Context of a Dependent Culture, *Occasional Papers,* no. 16 (New York University Ibero-American Language and Area Center, 1975), 2.

5. H. Hoetink, *Slavery and Race Relations in the Americas* (New York: Harper and Row, 1973), 130.
6. Leopoldo Zea, "Negritud e indigenismo," *Cuadernos americanos* 197 (1974): 16–30.
7. Roberto Fernández Retamar, *Ensayo de otro mundo* (Santiago: Editorial Universitaria, 1969), 115.
8. Sánchez, "Three Latin American Novelists in Search of *Lo Americano,* 76.
9. Ibid., 144.
10. Ibid.
11. Gordon Brotherston, "Vernacular American," in *Latin American Poetry: Origins and Presence* (Cambridge: Cambridge University Press, 1975), 7–26.
12. Rodríquez Monegal, "Metamorphoses of Caliban," 78–83.
13. Jean Franco, *The Modern Culture of Latin America: Society and the Artist* (Middlesex, England: Penguin Books, 1970), 42.
14. Harss and Dohman, *Into the Mainstream,* 41.
15. D. P. Gallagher, *Modern Latin American Literature* (London: Oxford University Press, 1973), 83.
16. Ibid., 83.
17. Jean Franco, "Criticism and Literature," 6.
18. Ibid.
19. Ibid.
20. J. B. Kubayanda, "Afrocentric Hermeneutics and the Rhetoric of *transculturación* in Black Latin American Literature," in *Latin America and the Caribbean: Geopolitics, Development, and Culture* (Ottawa: Calacs, 1983), 226–40.
21. Nelson Estupiñán Bass, *Timarán y Cuabú* (Quito: Editorial Casa de la Cultura Ecuatoriana, 1956).
22. Nelson Estupiñán Bass, *El desempate* (Portoviejo, Ecuador: Editorial Gregorio, 1980). Estupiñán Bass expects to publish this volume and *Timarán y Cuabú* together as *Duelo de gigantes.*
23. Estupiñán Bass, *Timarán y Cuabú,* 80.
24. Estupiñán Bass, *El desempate,* 20.
25. Ibid., 92.
26. Estupiñán Bass, *Timarán y Cuabú,* 9.
27. Nelson Estupiñán Bass, *El desempate,* 91.
28. Ibid., 97.
29. Franco, "Criticism and Literature," 6.
30. Ibid.

31. Addison Gayle, Jr., "The Function of Black Criticism at the Present Time," in *Reading Black: Essays in the Criticism of African, Caribbean, and Black American Literature*, ed. Houston A. Baker, Jr. (Ithaca: Cornell University Africana Studies and Research Center, 1976), 37.

32. Lemuel Johnson, "Issues in the Aesthetics of Populism and a Black Aesthetic" (Paper presented at the National Council for Black Studies Conference, Ohio State University, Columbus, Ohio, February 16–19, 1977), 5.

33. Richard K. Barksdale, "Humanistic Protest in Recent Black Poetry," in *Modern Black Poets: A Collection of Critical Essays*, ed. Donald B. Gibson (Englewood Cliffs, N.J.: Prentice-Hall, 1973), 159.

34. Ibid., 164.

35. Léopold Sédar Senghor, *Négritude et humanisme* (Paris, Éditiones du Seuil, 1964).

36. Albert Gérard, "Humanism and Negritude: Notes on the Contemporary Afro-American Novel," *Diogenes* 37 (1962), 120.

37. Ibid., 120.

38. See *Negritude: Black Poetry from Africa and the Caribbean*, ed. and trans. Norman R. Shapiro (New York: October House, 1970).

39. Gunter Lorenz, "Adalberto Ortiz," in *Diálogo con América Latina* (Valparaíso: Ediciones Universitarias de Valparaíso, 1972), 319–32.

40. J. Gallegos Lara, "Raza, poesía, y novela de Adalberto Ortiz," prologue to Ortiz's *El animal herido* (Quito: Casa de la Cultura Ecuatoriana, 1959), 13–20.

41. Carl Pederson, Jr., "Main Trends in the Contemporary Colombian Novel, 1953–1967" (Ph.D. diss., University of Southern California, 1971), 265.

42. René Dépestre, "Orfeo negro", in *Recopilación de textos sobre Nicolás Guillén*, ed. Nancy Morejón (Havana: Casa de las Américas, 1974), 121–25.

43. Keith Ellis, "Nicolás Guillén at Seventy," *Caribbean Quarterly* 19, no. 3 (1973): 87–94.

44. Keith Ellis, "Literary Americanism and the Recent Poetry of Nicolás Guillén," *University of Toronto Quarterly* 45, no. 1 (1976): 14.

45. Lorna Williams, "Nicolás Guillén and the Poetic Response to the Cuban Revolution" (Paper read at a Seminar in Atlantic History and Culture at Johns Hopkins University, February 27, 1979).

46. Ibid., 4.

47. G. R. Coulthard, "Nicolás Guillén and West Indian Negritude," *Caribbean Quarterly* 16, no. 1 (1970): 57.

48. James Irish, "Notes on a Historic Visit: Nicolás Guillén in Jamaica," *Caribbean Quarterly* 21 (1975): 74.
49. In "El poeta Nicolás Guillén, de paso por Madrid," *ABC* (July 24, 1970): 45.
50. In Osvaldo Navarro, "Guillén, joven también," *El caimán barbudo* (March 1977), 13.
51. Keith Ellis, "Literary Americanism," 11.
52. José Antonio Portuondo, "Prologue," in *Tengo,* trans. Richard Carr (Detroit: Broadside Press, 1974), 16.
53. Martha Cobb, "Redefining the Definitions in Afro-Hispanic Literature," *College Language Association Journal* 23, no. 2 (1979): 158.
54. David Brookshaw, *Race and Color in Brazilian Literature,* 217.
55. Ibid., 218.
56. Ibid., 229.
57. Lorna Williams, *Self and Society in the Poetry of Nicolás Guillén* (Baltimore: Johns Hopkins University Press, 1982), 42.

Five. The Continuing Quest

1. Ian Smart, "Religious Elements in the Narrative of Quince Duncan," *Afro-Hispanic Review* 1, no. 2 (1982): 30.
2. Ibid., 29.
3. Carlos Guillermo Wilson ("Cubena"), *Chombo* (Miami: Ediciones Universal, 1981), 83.
4. Carlos Guillermo Wilson ("Cubena"), *Afroexiliados,* 6. All subsequent page references are to the manuscript copy.
5. Carlos Guillermo Wilson ("Cubena"), *Chombo,* 206.
6. Lorna Williams, "Carlos Guillermo Wilson and the Dialectics of Ethnicity in Panama," *Afro-Hispanic Review* 4, nos. 2–3 (1985): 14.
7. Ibid., 15.
8. Nelson Estupiñán Bass to the author, June 5, 1978.
9. Nelson Estupiñán Bass, *Senderos brillantes* (Quito: Editorial Casa de la Cultura Ecuatoriana, 1974), 243.
10. Estupiñán Bass to the author, June 5, 1978.
11. Luys A. Díez, "Another Chapter of Peru's *Comedie Grotesque,*" *Review* 23 (1978): 59.

12. Nelson Estupiñán Bass, *Toque de queda* (Guayaquil: Casa de la Cultura Ecuatoriana, 1978), 67.

13. Nelson Estupiñán Bass, *Bajo el cielo nublado* (Quito: Editorial Casa de la Cultura Ecuatoriana, 1981), 229.

14. Nelson Estupiñán Bass expects to publish this novel, which I read in manuscript, in Ecuador in the very near future.

15. Henry J. Richards, "Entrevista con Nelson Estupiñán Bass." *Afro-Hispanic Review* 4, nos. 2–3 (1985): 34.

16. Ellis, "Literary Americanism," 7.

17. Mario Vargas Llosa, "The Genesis and Evolution of *Pantaleón y las visitadoras*," ed. and trans. Raquel Chang-Rodríquez and Gabriella de Beer, *The City College Papers*, no. 12 (New York: The City College, 1979), 24.

18. Estupiñán Bass, *Toque de queda*, 195.

19. Estupiñán Bass, *Senderos brillantes*, 238.

20. Estupiñán Bass, *Toque de queda*, 69.

21. Jorge Artel, *No es la muerte, es el morir* (Bogotá: Ecoe Ediciones, 1979).

22. Juan Zapata Olivella, *Historia de un joven negro* (Port-au-Prince: Edicion Hatiana Le Natal, 1983).

23. Juan Zapata Olivella, *Pisando el camino de ébano* (Bogotá: Ediciones Lerner, 1984).

Six. The Shango Saga

1. All references to this early work are to the following edition: Manuel Zapata Olivella, *He visto la noche* (Medellin, Colombia: Editorial Bedout, 1974).

2. Leonard E. Barrett, *Soul-Force: African Heritage in Afro-American Religion* (Garden City, N.Y.: Doubleday, 1974), 17.

3. Migene González-Wippler, *Santería: African Magic in Latin America* (Garden City, N.Y.: Doubleday, 1975), 105.

4. Barrett, *Soul-Force*, 21.

5. Janheinz Jahn, *Muntu: An Outline of the New African Culture*, trans. Majorie Grene (New York: Grove Press, 1961), 66.

6. Lillian Cleamons Franklin, "The Image of the Black in the Cuban Theatre, 1913–1965" (Ph.D. diss., Ohio State University, 1982), 271.

7. Julia C. Hewitt, "Yoruba Presence in Contemporary Cuban Narrative" (Ph.D. diss., Vanderbilt University, 1981), 136.

8. Manuel Zapata Olivella, Changó, el gran putas (Bogotá: La oveja negra, 1983), 158.

9. Yvonne Captain-Hidalgo, "Conversación con el doctor Manuel Zapata Olivella," Afro-Hispanic Review 4, no. 1 (1985): 30.

10. Barrett, Soul-Force, 22 and 23.

11. Manuel Zapata Olivella, Changó, 95.

12. Ian Smart, review of Changó, el gran putas, by Manuel Zapata Olivella, Afro-Hispanic Review 3, no. 2 (1984): 32; also, see his "Changó, el gran putas, una nueva novela poemática," in Ensayos de literatura colombiana, ed. Raymond L. Williams (Bogotá: Plaza y Janes, 1985), 149–56.

13. See Yvonne Captain-Hidalgo, "The Realm of Possible Realities: A Comparative Analysis of Selected Works by Alejo Carpentier and Manuel Zapata Olivella" (Ph.D. diss., Stanford University, 1984), and her "El espacio del tiempo en Changó, el gran putas," in Ensayos de literatura colombiana, ed. Raymond L. Williams (Bogotá: Plaza y Janes, 1985), 157–63.

14. Miguel Barnet, "The Culture That Sugar Cane Created," Latin American Literary Review 8, no. 16 (1980): 41.

15. Smart, "Religious Elements in the Narrative of Quince Duncan," 30.

16. Quince Duncan, "Los mitos ancestrales," in La rebelión pocomía y otros relatos (San José: Editorial Costa Rica, 1976), 73–91.

17. See Antonio Olinto, "The Negro Writer and the Negro Influence in Brazilian Literature," African Forum 2, no. 4 (1967): 18.

18. Captain-Hidalgo, "Conversación con el doctor Manuel Zapata Olivella," 30.

19. Rosalía Cortés, "L'epopée du noir dans le nouveau monde selon Manuel Zapata Olivella," Notre Librairie 80 (July–Sept. 1985): 99.

20. Gilberto Gómez and Raymond L. Williams, "Interview with Manuel Zapata Olivella," Hispania 67 (Dec. 1984): 657.

Seven. Toward a Human Poetics

1. Julius Lester, "Growing Down," Change 2 (1979): 79.

2. Franck Bayard, "The Black Latin American Impact on Western Culture," in The Negro Impact on Western Civilization, ed. Joseph S. Roucek and Thomas Kierman (New York: Philosophical Library, 1970), 293.

3. Ibid., 297.

4. Ibid.

5. Ibid., 302.

6. Robert B. Stepto, "Teaching Afro-American Literature: Survey or Tradition," in *Afro-American Literature: The Reconstruction of Instruction*, ed. Dexter Fisher and Robert B. Stepto (New York: Modern Language Association, 1979), 23.

7. Ibid.

8. Murray Krieger, *Theory of Criticism: A Tradition and Its System* (Baltimore: Johns Hopkins University Press, 1976), xiii.

9. Jeffrey Sammons, *Literary Sociology and Practical Criticism: An Inquiry* (Bloomington: Indiana University Press, 1977), 140.

10. Ibid., 156.

11. Quentin G. Kraft, "Science and Poetics, Old and New," *College English* 37 (1975): 171.

12. Addison Gayle, Jr., ed., *The Black Aesthetic* (Garden City, N.Y.: Doubleday, 1971), xxiii.

13. Eugene Goodheart, *The Failure of Criticism* (Cambridge: Harvard University Press, 1978), 4.

14. John Gardner, *On Moral Fiction* (New York: Basic Books, 1978).

15. John Reichert, *Making Sense of Literature* (Chicago: University of Chicago Press, 1977), 55–95.

16. Ibid., 173–204.

17. Germaine Brée, "Literary Analysis: Today's Mandarins," in *The Analysis of Hispanic Texts: Current Trends in Methodology*, ed. Lisa E. Davis and Isabel C. Tarán (New York: Bilingual Press, 1976), 9.

18. Sammons, *Literary Sociology*, 177.

19. Ibid.

20. Gardner, *On Moral Fiction*, 145.

21. Fisher and Stepto, *Afro-American Literature*, 175.

22. Ibid., 236.

23. Tittler, "*Juyungo*/Reading Writing," in *Voices from Under*, 177.

24. Henry Lewis Gates, Jr., "Preface to Blackness: Text and Pretext," in Fisher and Stepto, *Afro-American Literature*, 66.

25. Lester, "Growing Down," 37.

26. Ibid.

27. Ibid., 34.

28. Emile Snyder, "The Problem of Negritude in Modern French Poetry," *Com-*

parative Literature Studies, special issue, edited by Haskell M. Block (1963): 101.

29. Lester, "Growing Down," 37.

30. Albert Gérard, "Humanism and Negritude: Notes on the Contemporary Afro-American Novel," *Diogenes* 37 (1962): 124.

31. C. L. Innes, "Through the Looking Glass: African and Irish Nationalist Writing," in *African Literature Today,* no. 9 (1978): 11.

Bibliography

General Literature

Anderson Imbert, Enrique. *Crítica interna*. Madrid: Ediciones Taurus, 1960.
_____. *Métodos de crítica literaria*. Madrid: Editorial Revista de Occidente, 1969.
Baquero Goyanes, M. *Estructuras de la novela*. Barcelona: Editorial Planeta, 1970.
Benamou, Michel. "The Concept of Marginality in Ethnopoetics." In *Minority Language and Literature*, edited by Dexter Fisher. New York: Modern Language Association, 1977.
Bleich, David. *Subjective Criticism*. Baltimore: Johns Hopkins University Press, 1978.
Booth, Wayne. *The Rhetoric of Fiction*. Chicago: University of Chicago Press, 1966.
Brée, Germaine. "Literary Analysis: Today's Mandarins." In *The Analysis of Hispanic Texts: Current Trends in Methodology*, edited by Lisa E. Davis and Isabel C. Tarán, 1–10. New York: Bilingual Press, 1976.
Bush, Douglas. "The Humanist Critic." *The Kenyon Review* 13, no. 1 (1951): 81–92.
Castignino, Raul H. *El análisis literario: Introducción metodológica a una estilística integral*. Buenos Aires: Editorial Nova, 1974.
Culler, Jonathan. *Structuralist Poetics*. London: Routledge and Kegan Paul, 1975.
Daiches, David. *Critical Approaches to Literature*. New York: W. W. Norton and Co., 1956.
Davis, Walter. *The Act of Interpretation: A Critique of Literary Reason*. Chicago: University of Chicago Press, 1978.
Eco, Humberto. *A Theory of Semiotics*. Bloomington: Indiana University Press, 1976.
Foester, Norman. "The Esthetic Judgement and the Ethical Judgement." In *The*

Intent of the Critic, edited and with an introduction by Donald A. Stauffer, 52–72. New York: Bantam, 1941.

Forster, E. M. *Aspects of the Novel.* 1927. Reprint. Middlesex, England: Penguin Books, 1958.

Foster, Richard. "Reflections on Teaching Criticism." In *Criticism,* edited by L. S. Dembo, 143–44. Madison: University of Wisconsin Press, 1968.

Fowler, Roger. *Linguistics and the Novel.* London: Methuen and Co., 1977.

Friedman, Alan W. *The Moral Quality of Form in the Modern Novel.* Baton Rouge: Louisiana State University Press, 1978.

Friedman, Norman. *Form and Meaning in Fiction.* Athens: University of Georgia Press, 1975.

Frye, Northrop. *Anatomy of Criticism: Four Essays.* Princeton, N.J.: Princeton University Press, 1957.

Gardner, John. *On Moral Fiction.* New York: Basic Books, 1978.

Garrido Gallardo, M. A. *Introducción a la teoría de la literatura.* Madrid: Sociedad General Española de Librería, 1975.

Goldman, Lucien. *Towards a Sociology of the Novel.* Translated from the French by Alan Sheridan. London: Tavistock Publications, 1975.

Goodheart, Eugene. *The Failure of Criticism.* Cambridge: Harvard University Press, 1978.

Graff, Gerald. *Literature against Itself: Literary Ideas in Modern Society.* Chicago: University of Chicago Press, 1979.

Guerin, Wilfred, L., et al., *A Handbook of Critical Approaches to Literature.* New York: Harper and Row, 1966.

Gullón, Germán, and Agnes Gullón, eds. *Teoría de la novela.* Madrid: Taurus Ediciones, 1974.

Halperin, John, ed. *The Theory of the Novel: New Essays.* New York: Oxford University Press, 1974.

Handy, William J. *Modern Fiction: A Formalistic Approach.* Carbondale: Southern Illinois University Press, 1971.

Hawkes, Terrence. *Structuralism and Semiotics.* London: Methuen and Co., 1977.

Hirch, E. D., Jr. *Validity in Interpretation.* New Haven: Yale University Press, 1967.

Ingarden, Roman. *The Literary Work of Art.* Translated by George G. Grabowicz. Evanston, Ill.: Northwestern University Press, 1973.

James, Henry. *The Art of the Novel (1907–1917).* New York: Charles Scribner's Sons, 1962.

Kayser, Wolfgang. *Interpretación y análisis de la obra literaria.* Translated by María D. Mouton and V. García Yebra. Madrid: Editorial Gredos, 1961.

Kraft, Quentin G. "Science and Poetics, Old and New." *College English* 37 (1975): 167–97.

Krieger, Murray. *Theory of Criticism: A Tradition and Its Systems.* Baltimore: Johns Hopkins University Press, 1976.

Kuma, F. M. "Literature and the Teaching of Literature: Observations on Literary Form." In *The Uses of Criticism,* edited by A. P. Foulkes et al., 193–202. Frankfurt: M. Peter Lang, 1976.

Leavis, F. R. *Common Pursuit.* Middlesex, England: Penguin, 1952.

Lukas, Georg. *Studies in European Realism.* New York: Grosset and Dunlap, 1964.

———. *The Theory of the Novel.* Translated by Anna Bostock. Cambridge, Mass.: M.I.T. Press, 1971.

McGlynn, Paul, "Social and Literary Values and their Analogical Resemblances." In *Criticism and Culture,* edited by Sherman Paul, 32–37. Iowa City: Midwest Language Association, 1972.

McGraw, B. R. "Barthes' *The Pleasure of the Text:* An Erotics of Reading." *Boundary 2* 5 (1977): 943–52.

Maritain, Jacques. *Integral Humanism.* Translated by Joseph W. Evans. Notre Dame, Ind.: University of Notre Dame Press, 1973.

Miller, James E., ed. *Myth and Method: Modern Theories of Fiction.* Lincoln: University of Nebraska Press, 1960.

Ortega y Gasset, José. *The Dehumanization of Art.* Garden City, N.Y.: Doubleday and Co., 1956.

Quasha, George. "The Age of the Secret." In *Alcheringa,* edited by Michel Benamou and Jerome Rothenberg. Boston: Boston University, 1976.

Reichert, John. *Making Sense of Literature.* Chicago: University of Chicago Press, 1977.

Richards, I. A. *Practical Criticism: A Study of Literary Judgements.* New York: Harcourt, Brace and World, 1979.

Said, Edward W. *Beginnings: Intentions and Method.* Baltimore: Johns Hopkins University Press, 1975.

Sammons, Jeffrey L. *Literary Sociology and Practical Criticism: An Inquiry.* Bloomington: Indiana University Press, 1977.

Sanz Villanueva, S., and C. J. Barbachano, eds. *Teoría de la novela.* Madrid: Sociedad General Española de Librería, 1976.

Sawhill, John C. "The Unlettered University." *Harper's,* February 1979, 35–40.

Scholes, Robert, ed. *Approaches to the Novel: Materials for a Poetics.* San Francisco: Chandler Publishing Co., 1961.

————. *Structuralism in Literature: An Introduction.* New Haven: Yale University Press, 1974.

Schorer, Mark. "Technique As Discovery." *Hudson Review* (1948). Reprinted in *Approaches to the Novel: Materials for a Poetics,* edited by Robert Scholes, 249–68. San Francisco: Chandler Publishing Co., 1961.

Scott, Wilson. *Five Approaches of Literary Criticism.* London: Collier Books, 1962.

Segre, Cesare. *Semiotics and Literary Criticism.* The Hague: Mouton, 1973.

Shumaker, Wayne. "A Modest Proposal for Critics." In *Criticism,* edited by L. S. Dembo. Madison: University of Wisconsin Press, 1968.

Sontag, Susan. *Against Interpretation.* New York: Dell Publishing Co., 1961.

Spilka, Mark, ed. *Towards a Poetics of Fiction.* Bloomington: Indiana University Press, 1977.

Stevick, Philip, ed. *The Theory of the Novel.* New York: Free Press, 1967.

Tacca, Oscar. *Las voces de la novela.* Madrid: Editorial Gredos, 1973.

Tennenhouse, Leonard, ed. *The Practice of Psychoanalytic Criticism.* Detroit: Wayne State University Press, 1976.

Tomashevsky, Boris. "Thematics." In *Russian Formalistic Criticism: Four Essays,* 61–95. Translated with an introduction by Lee T. Lemon and Marion J. Reis. Lincoln: University of Nebraska Press, 1965.

Torre, Guillermo de. *Nuevas direcciones de la crítica literaria.* Madrid: Alianza Editorial, 1970.

Towers, Robert. "Good Grief." *The New York Review of Books,* July 20, 1978, 30–31.

Wade, Ira. "Criticism as Humanistic Art." In *Directions of Literary Criticism in the Seventies,* edited by Donald W. Bleznick and John F. Turner, 1–17. Cincinnati: University of Cincinnati, Department of Romance Languages, 1972.

Wellek, René, and Austin Warren. *Theory of Literature.* New York: Harcourt, Brace and Co., 1956.

White, Hayden. "The Absurdist Movement in Contemporary Literary Theory." In *Directions for Criticism: Structuralism and Its Alternatives,* edited by Murray Krieger and L. S. Dembo, 85–110. Madison: University of Wisconsin Press, 1977.

Latin American Literature

Adoum, Jorge Enrique. "El realismo de la otra realidad." In *América Latina en su literatura,* edited by César Fernández Moreno, 204–18. México: Siglo Veintiuno Editores, 1972.

Ainsa, Fernando. "La espiral abierta de la novela latinoamericana (notas para la construcción de un sistema novelesco)." In *Novelas hispanoamericanas de hoy,* edited by Juan Loveluck, 17–46. Madrid: Taurus, 1976.

Alegría, Fernando. *Historia de la novela hispanoamericana.* 3d ed. México: Ediciones de Andrea, 1966.

Amorós, Andrés. *Introducción a la novela hispanoamericana actual.* Salamanca: Ediciones Anaya, 1971.

Asturias, Miguel Angel. "Paisaje y lenguaje en la novela hispanoamericana." *Norte* 73 (1972): 61–69.

Benedetti, Mario. "El escritor y la crítica en el contexto del subdesarrollo." *Casa de las Américas,* no. 107 (1978): 3–21.

———. "Situación del intelectual en la América Latina." *Diez años de la Revista Casa de las Américas, 1960–1970"* 6 (1970): 150–54.

———. "Temas y Problemas." In *América Latina en su literatura,* edited by César Fernández Moreno, 354–71. Mexico: Siglo Veintiuno Editores, 1972.

Blanco Amor, José. *El final del boom literario y otros temas.* Buenos Aires: Ediciones Cervantes, 1976.

Blanco Aguinaga, Carlos. "Sobre la idea de la novela en Carlos Fuentes." Chapter 4 in *De mitólogos y novelistas.* Madrid: Ediciones Turner, 1975.

Brotherston, Gordon. *The Emergence of the Latin American Novel.* Cambridge: Cambridge University Press, 1977.

———. *Latin American Poetry: Origins and Presence.* Cambridge: Cambridge University Press, 1975.

Brushwood, John S. *The Spanish American Novel: A Twentieth-Century Survey.* Austin: University of Texas Press, 1975.

Cândido, Antonio. "Literatura y subdesarrollo." In *América Latina en su literatura,* edited by César Fernández Moreno, 335–53. México: Siglo Veintiuno Editores, 1972.

Carpentier, Alejo. *Literatura y conciencia política en América Latina.* Madrid: Alberto Corazón, 1969.

———. *Tientos y diferencias (ensayos).* México: Universidad Nacional Autónoma de México, 1964.

Centro de Estudios de Latinoamericanos. *Hacia una crítica literaria latinoamericana.* Buenos Aires: Fernando García Cambeiro, 1976.

Christ, Ronald. "Talk with Vargas Llosa." *New York Times Book Review,* April 9, 1978, 33.

Collazos, Oscar, et al. *Literatura en la revolución y revolución en la literatura.* México: Siglo Veintiuno Editores, 1970.

Cornejo Polar, Antonio. "El indigenismo y las literaturas heterogéneas: Su doble estatuto socio-cultural." *Revista de la crítica literaria,* año 7, nos. 7–8 (1978): 7–21.

Cortázar, Julio. "Novel Revolution." Translated by John Incledon. *Review* 24 (1979): 81–84.

Diez, Luys A. "Another Chapter of Peru's *Comedie Grotesque.*" *Review* 23 (1978): 54–61.

Donoso, José. *Historia personal del "boom."* Barcelona: Editorial Anagrama, 1972.

Ellis, Keith. *Critical Approaches to Rubén Darío.* Toronto: University of Toronto Press, 1974.

Fernández Moreno, César, ed. *América Latina en su literatura.* Mexico: Siglo Veintiuno Editores, 1972.

Fernández Retamar, Roberto. "Algunos problemas teóricos de la literatura hispanoamericana." *Revista de crítica literaria,* año 1, no. 1 (1975): 7–38.

———. "Algunos usos de civilización y barbarie." *Casa de las Américas,* no. 102 (1977): 29–52.

———. *Calibán: Apuntes sobre la cultura en nuestra América.* México: Editorial Diógenes, 1921. Translated by Lynn Garafola et al. as "Caliban: Notes Toward a Discussion of Culture in Our America." *Massachusetts Review* 15 (1974): 7–72.

———. "Contra la leyenda negra." *Casa de las Américas.* 99 (1976): 28–41.

———. *Ensayo de otro mundo.* Santiago: Editorial Universitaria, 1969.

———. *Para una teoría de la literatura hispanoamericana y otras aproximaciones.* Havana: Casa de las Américas, 1975.

Foster, David William. *Currents in the Contemporary Argentine Novel.* Columbia: University of Missouri Press, 1975.

Franco, Jean. *César Vallejo: The Dialectics of Poetry and Silence.* Cambridge: Cambridge University Press, 1976.

———. "The Crisis of the Liberal Imagination." *Ideologies and Literature* 1 (December 1976–January 1977): 5–24.

———. "Criticism and Literature within the Context of a Dependent Culture."

Occasional Paper no. 16. New York University Ibero-American Language and Area Center, 1975.

_____. *The Modern Culture of Latin America: Society and the Artist.* Middlesex, England: Penguin Books, 1970.

_____. *Spanish American Literature since Independence.* London: Ernest Benn, 1973.

Fuentes, Carlos. *La nueva novela hispanoamericana.* México: Joaquín Mortiz, 1969.

Gallagher, D. P. *Modern Latin American Literature.* London: Oxford University Press, 1973.

García Márquez, Gabriel, and Mario Vargas Llosa. *La novela en América Latina: Diálogo.* Lima: Milla Batres, 1968.

Gertel, Zunilda. *La novela hispanoamericana contemporánea.* Buenos Aires: Editorial Colomba, 1971.

Goic, Cedomil. *Historia de la novela hispanoamericana.* Valparaíso, Chile: Ediciones Universitarias de Valparaíso, 1972.

González, Alfonso. "Narrative Techniques in Twentieth-Century Spanish American *novomundismo.*" In *Graduate Studies in Latin America at the University of Kansas,* vol. 1, edited by Charles L. Stansifer, 53–62. Lawrence: University of Kansas, 1973.

González, Manuel Pedro. "La novela hispanoamericana en el contexto de lo internacional." In *Coloquio sobre la novela hispanoamericana,* edited by Ivan A. Schulman et al., 35–109. Mexico: Tezontle, 1967.

González Echevarría, Roberto. *Alejo Carpentier: The Pilgrim at Home.* Ithaca: Cornell University Press, 1978.

Graña, César. *Fact and Symbol: Essays in the Sociology of Art and Literature.* New York: Oxford University Press, 1971.

Grases, Pedro. "De la novela en América." *Mesa rodante* 1 (1949): 9–17. Reprinted in *La novela hispanoamericana,* 2d ed., edited by Juan Loveluck, 97–105. Santiago de Chile: Editorial Universitaria, 1966.

Gutiérrez Giradot, Rafael. "Tesis para una sociología de la literatura hispanoamericana." In *Literatura de la emancipación hispanoamericana y otros ensayos,* Proceedings of the Fifteenth Congress of the Institute of Iberoamerican Literature, 108–13. Lima: Universidad Nacional Mayor de San Marcos, 1972.

Harss, Luis. *Los nuestros.* Buenos Aires: Editorial Sudamericana, 1966. Translated, with Barbara Dohman, as *Into the Mainstream: Conversations with Latin American Writers.* New York: Harper and Row, 1967.

Instituto Internacional de Literatura Iberoamericana. *La novela iberoamericana.*
Albuquerque: University of New Mexico Press, 1952.

_____. *La novela iberoamericana contemporánea.* Caracas: Universidad Central
de Venezuela, 1968.

Irish, James. "Magic Realism: A Search for Caribbean and Latin American
Roots." *Literary Half Yearly* 2 (1971): 127–39.

Janney, Frank. *Alejo Carpentier and His Early Works.* London: Tamesis Books,
1981.

Katra, William. "Cultural Dependency and Literature in Latin America." *Buckham Literary Studies: Michigan State University* 6 (1975): 1–9.

Kirk, John. "Post-'boom' Literature: What Can We Expect in the 1980s?" In
Latin American Prospects for the '80s: What kinds of Development? edited by
David Pollock and A. R. M. Ritter, 168–92. Ottawa: Norman Patterson
School of International Affairs, Carleton University, 1981.

Larson, Ross. *Fantasy and Imagination in the Mexican Narrative.* Tempe: Center
for Latin American Studies, Arizona State University, 1977.

Lazo, Raimundo. *La novela andina, pasado y futuro.* México: Porrúa, 1971.

Loveluck, Juan, ed. *La novela hispanoamericana.* 2d ed. Santiago de Chile:
Editorial Universitaria, 1969.

_____. *Novelistas hispanoamericanas de hoy.* Madrid: Taurus, 1976.

MacAdam, Alfred J. *Modern Latin American Narratives: The Dreams of Reason.*
Chicago: University of Chicago Press, 1977.

Mariátegui, José Carlos. *Seven Interpretative Essays on Peruvian Reality.* Translated
by Marjory Urquidi. Austin: University of Texas Press, 1971.

Martín, José Luis. *La narrativa de Vargas Llosa: Acercamiento estilístico.* Madrid:
Editorial Gredos, 1974.

Mead, Robert G., Jr. "After the Boom." *Américas* 30 (1978): 2–8.

Mejía Duque, Jaime. *Narrativa y neocolonialismo en América Latina.* Medellín
Colombia: Editorial La Oveja Negra, 1972.

Mörner, Magnus. *Race Mixture in the History of Latin America.* Boston: Little,
Brown and Co., 1967.

Novoa, Bruce. Introduction to "History According to Pao Cheng." *Latin American Literary Review,* 6, no. 12 (1978): 119–23.

Onís, Federico de. "Rubén Darío (1867–1916)." *La torre,* año 15, nos. 55 and
56 (Jan.–June 1967): 15–35.

Ortega, José. "Pablo Neruda: The Making of a Political Poet." In *Perspectives on
Contemporary Literature,* ed. Bonnie Reynolds, 3–11. Louisville: University of
Louisville Press, 1976.

Ospina, Uriel. *Problemas y perspectivas de la novela americana.* Bogotá: Ediciones Tercer Mundo, 1964.

Portuondo, José Antonio. "Criollo: definición y motivos de un concepto." *Hispania* 34 (1951): 172–76.

———. "El rasgo predominante en la novela hispanoamericana." In *La novela iberoamericana,* Proceedings of the Fifth International Congress of Iberoamerican Literature, 77–87. Albuquerque: University of New Mexico Press, 1951.

Rama, Angel. *Diez problemas para el novelista latinoamericano.* Caracas: Síntesis Dosmil, 1972.

Río, Roberto, ed. *La novela y el hombre hispanoamericano: El destino humano en la novela hispanoamericana contemporanea.* Buenos Aires: Nueva Imagen, 1969.

Roa Bastos, Augusto. "Imagen y perspectivas de la narrativa latinoamericana." In *Novelas hispanoamericanas de hoy,* edited by Juan Loveluck, 47–64. Madrid: Taurus, 1976.

Rodríquez Monegal, Emir. "The Metamorphoses of Caliban." *Diacritics* 7 (1977): 78–83.

Ruffinelli, Jorge. "La crítica literaria hoy." *Texto crítico: Revista del centro de investigaciones linguistico-literarias de la Universidad Veracruzana* 6 (1977): 3–36.

Sánchez, Luis Alberto. *América, novela sin novelistas.* 2d ed. Santiago de Chile: Editorial Ercilla, 1940.

———. *Proceso y contenido de la novela hispanoamericana.* 2d cd. Madrid: Editorial Gredos, 1968.

Sánchez, Marta. "Caliban: The New Latin American Protagonist of *The Tempest.*" *Diacritics* 6 (1976): 54–61.

———. "Three Latin American Novelists in Search of *Lo Americano:* A Productive Failure." Ph.D. diss., University of California, San Diego, 1977.

Schulman, Ivan A., et al. *Coloquio sobre la novela hispanoamericana.* México: Fondo de la Cultura Economica, 1967.

Schwartz, Kessel. *A New History of Spanish-American Fiction.* Vol. 1. Coral Gables, Fla.: University of Miami Press, 1972.

Segade, Gustav. "Central Issues in Contemporary Latin American Poetic Theory." Ph.D. diss., University of Arizona, 1972.

Siemens, William L. "Guillermo Cabrera Infante's *Tres tristes tigres.*" In *Graduate Studies on Latin America: The University of Kansas,* edited by Charles L. Stansifer, 75–86. Lawrence: University of Kansas, 1973.

Spell, Jefferson Rea. *Contemporary Spanish-American Fiction.* Chapel Hill, North Carolina: University of North Carolina Press, 1944.

Squirru, Rafael. "Into the Mainstream: Conversations with Latin American Writers." *Américas,* 19 (June 1967): 44.

Torres Rioseco, Arturo. *Grandes novelistas de la América Hispana.* Berkeley: University of California Press, 1941.

————. *Novelistas contemporáneos de América.* Santiago de Chile: Editorial Nascimento, 1939.

Valdivieso, M. Jaime. *Realidad y ficción en Latinoamérica.* Mexico: Editorial Joaquín Mortiz, 1975.

Vargas Llosa, Mario. "The Genesis and Evolution of *Pantaleón y las visitadoras.*" Edited and translated by Raquel Chang-Rodríquez and Gabriella de Beer. *The City College Papers,* no. 12. New York: The City College, 1979.

————. "The Latin American Novel Today: Introduction." *Books Abroad* 44, no. 1 (1970): 7–16.

————. "Luzbel, Europa y otras conspiraciones." In *Literatura en revolución y revolución en la literatura,* edited by Oscar Collazos, 78–93. México: Siglo Veintiuno Editores, 1970.

————. "La novela primitiva y la novela de creación en América Latina." *Revista de la Universidad de México* 23, no. 10 (1969): 29–33. In English, "Primitives and Creators." *Times Literary Supplement,* Nov. 14, 1968, 1287–88.

————. "Social Commitment and the Latin American Writer," *World Literature Today* (formerly *Books Abroad*) 58 (1978): 5–14.

Vergara, Ricardo. *La novela hispanoamericana, descubrimiento e invención de América.* Valparaíso: Ediciones Universitarias de Valparaíso, 1973.

Verzasconi, Ray. "Magical Realism and the Literary World of Miguel Angel Asturias." Ph.D. diss., University of Washington, 1965.

Vidal, Hernán. *Literatura hispanoamericana e ideología liberal: Surgimiento y crisis (una problemática sobre la dependencia en torno a la narración del boom).* Buenos Aires: Ediciones Hispamérica, 1976.

Xirau, Ramón. "Crisis del realismo." In *América Latina en su literatura,* edited by César Fernández Moreno, 185–203. México: Siglo Veintiuno Editores, 1972.

Yudice, George. "The Poetics of Breakdown." *Review* 23 (1978): 20–24.

Zum Felde, Alberto. *Indice crítico de la literatura hispanoamericana.* Vol. 2, *La narrativa.* México, D. F.: Editorial Guaranía, 1959.

Black Literature in the Americas

Aguirre, Mirta. "El cincuentenario de *Motivos de son.*" Introduction to Nicolás Guillén, *Motivos de son.* Havana: Editorial Letras Cubanas, 1980.

Augier, Angel. *Nicolás Guillén: Notas para un estudio biográfico-crítico.* Vol. 1. Havana: Universidad Central de las Villas, 1962.

Baker, Houston A., Jr. "On the Criticism of Black American Literature: One View of the Black Aesthetic." In *Reading Black: Essays in the Criticism of African, Caribbean, and Black American Literature.* Cornell University Africana Studies and Research Center Monograph Series, no. 4, edited by Houston A. Baker, 48–58. Ithaca, 1976.

Baldwin, James. *The Fire Next Time.* New York: Dial Press, 1965.

Ballester, Marisol. "Three Possibilities for Black Liberation in *Juyungo.*" *Afro-Hispanic Review* 2, no. 2 (1983): 5–8.

Barksdale, Richard K. "Humanistic Protest in Recent Black Poetry." In *Modern Black Poets: A Collection of Critical Essays,* edited by Donald B. Gibson, 157–64. Englewood Cliffs, N.J.: Prentice-Hall, 1973.

Barnet, Miguel. "The Culture That Sugar Cane Created." *Latin American Review* 8 (1980): 38–46.

Barradas, Efraín. "Cigarro, Colón: Ciclón: Ciclo: Nota para una relectura de *Ecué Yambá O.*" *Sin nombre* 12, no. 2 (1981): 81–95.

Barrett, Leonard. *Soul-Force: African Heritage in Afro-American Religion.* Garden City, N.Y.: Doubleday and Co., 1974.

Bayard, Franck. "The Black Latin American Impact on Western Culture." In *The Negro Impact on Western Civilization,* edited by Joseph S. Roucek and Thomas Kierman, 337–60. New York: Philosophical Library, 1970.

Beane, Carol. "The Characterization of Blacks and Mulattoes in Selected Novels from Colombia, Venezuela, Ecuador, and Peru." Ph.D. diss., University of California, Berkeley, 1980.

Boyd, Antonio Olliz. "The Concept of Black Esthetics As Seen in Selected Works of Three Latin American Writers: Machado de Assis, Nicolás Guillén, and Adalberto Ortiz." Ph.D. diss., Stanford University, 1975.

Brookshaw, David. *Race and Color in Brazilian Literature.* Metuchen, N.J.: Scarecrow Press, 1986.

Brookshaw, Michael, "Protest, Militancy, and Revolution: The Evolution of the Afro-Hispanic Novel of the Diaspora." Ph.D. diss., University of Illinois at Urbana-Champaign, 1983.

Captain-Hidalgo, Yvonne. "Conversación con el doctor Manuel Zapata Olivella." *Afro-Hispanic Review* 4, no. 1 (1985): 26–32.

———. "El espacio del tiempo en *Changó, el gran putas.*" In *Ensayos de literatura colombiana,* edited by Raymond L. Williams, 157–63. Bogotá: Plaza y Janes, 1985.

———. "The Realm of Possible Realities: A Comparative Analysis of Selected Works by Alejo Carpentier and Manuel Zapata Olivella." Ph.D. diss., Stanford University, 1984.

Cauley, Anne. "A Definition of Freedom in the Fiction of Richard Wright." *College Language Association Journal* 19, no. 3 (1976): 327–46.

Cobb, Martha. "Afro-Arabs, Blackamoors, and Blacks: An Inquiry into Race Concepts through Spanish Literature." In *Blacks in Hispanic Literature,* edited by Miriam DeCosta, 20–28. Port Washington, N.Y.: Kennikat Press, 1977.

———. "Concepts of Blackness in the Poetry of Nicolás Guillén, Jacques Roumain, and Langston Hughes." *College Language Association Journal* 18, no. 2 (1974): 262–72.

———. *Harlem, Haiti, and Havana: A Comparative Study of Langston Hughes, Jacques Roumain, and Nicolás Guillén.* Washington, D.C.: Three Continents Press, 1979.

———. "Ortiz, Glissant, and Ellison: Fictional Patterns in Black Literature." *Afro-Hispanic Review* 1, no. 3 (1982): 5–9.

———. "Redefining the Definitions in Afro-Hispanic Literature." *College Language Association Journal* 23, no. 2 (1979): 147–59.

Collier, Eugenia. "Steps Towards a Black Aesthetic: A Study of Black American Literary Criticism." Ph.D. diss., University of Maryland, 1977.

Cortés, Rosalía. "L'épopée du noir dans le nouveau monde selon Manuel Zapata Olivella." *Notre Librairie,* 80 (July–Sept. 1985): 99–100.

Coulthard, G. R. "Nicolás Guillén and West Indian Negritude." *Caribbean Quarterly* 16, no. 1 (1970): 52–57.

———. "Parallelisms and Divergencies Between 'Negritude' and 'Indigenismo.'" *Caribbean Studies* 8, no. 1 (1968): 31–55.

———. *Race and Colour in Caribbean Literature.* London: Oxford University Press, 1962.

Dash, Michael. "Marvellous Realism: The Way Out of Negritude." *Black Images* 3, no. 1 (1974): 80–95.

Davis-Lett, Stephanie. "Blacks and *Criollismo:* A Curious Relationship." *College Language Association Journal* 24, no. 2 (1980): 131–49.

Dépestre, René. "Orfeo negro." In *Recopilación de textos sobre Nicolás Guillén*, edited by Nancy Morejón, 121–25. Havana: Casa de las Américas, 1974.

———. "Problems of Identity for the Black Man in Caribbean Literature." *Caribbean Quarterly* 19 (1973): 51–61.

Dunzo, Annette Ivory. "Black Heroes in the Theater of Early Spain." In *Homenaje a Lydia Cabrera*, edited by Reinaldo Sánchez et al. Miami: Ediciones Universal, 1978.

———. "Blacks of Sub-Saharan African Origin in Spain: Image in the Theater, 1500–1700," Ph.D. diss., U.C.L.A., 1974.

Ellis, Keith, Cuba's *Nicolás Guillén: Poetry and Ideology.* Toronto: University of Toronto Press, 1983.

———. "Literary Americanism and the Recent Poetry of Nicolás Guillén." *University of Toronto Quarterly* 45, no. 1 (1976): 1–18.

———. "Nicolás Guillén at Seventy." *Caribbean Quarterly* 19, no. 3 (1973): 87–94.

Farrison, Edward. Review of *Invisible Poets: Afro-Americans of the Nineteenth Century,* by Joan Sherman. *College Language Association Journal* 18, no. 2 (1974): 306.

Fisher, Dexter, and Robert B. Stepto, eds. *Afro-American Literature: The Reconstruction of Instruction.* New York: Modern Language Association, 1979.

Franklin, Lillian Cleamons. "The Image of the Black in the Cuban Theater, 1913–1965." Ph.D. diss., Ohio State University, 1982.

Gallegos Lara, J. "Raza, poesía y novela de Adalberto Ortiz." Prologue to *El animal herido,* by Adalberto Ortiz. Quito: Casa de la Cultura Ecuatoriana, 1959.

Gayle, Addison, Jr., ed. *The Black Aesthetic.* Garden City, N.Y.: Doubleday and Co., 1971.

———. "The Function of Black Criticism at the Present Time." In *Reading Black: Essays in the Criticism of African, Caribbean, and Black American Literature.* Cornell University Africana Studies and Research Center Monograph Series, no. 4, edited by Houston A. Baker, 37–40. Ithaca, 1976.

Gérard, Albert. "Humanism and Negritude: Notes on the Contemporary Afro-American Novel." *Diogenes,* no. 37 (Spring 1962): 115–33.

Gómez, Gilberto, and Raymond L. Williams. "Interview with Manuel Zapata Olivella," *Hispania* 67 (Dec. 1984): 657–58.

González-Wippler, Migene. *Santería: African Magic in Latin America.* Garden City, N.Y.: Doubleday and Co., 1975.

Guillén, Nicolás. "El camino de Harlem." In *Prosa de prisa, 1929–1972*. Vol. 1, 3–6. Havana: Editorial Arte y Literatura, 1975.

———. "Cuba, negros, poesía: Esquema para un ensayo." In *Prosa de prisa, 1929–1972*. Vol. 1, 94–101. Havana: Editorial Arte y Literatura, 1975.

Hemenway, Robert. "Are You a Flying Lark or a Setting Dove?" In *Afro-American Literature: The Reconstruction of Instruction*, edited by Dexter Fisher and Robert B. Stepto, 122–52. New York: Modern Language Association, 1979.

Hewitt, Julia C. "Yoruba Presence in Contemporary Cuban Narrative." Ph.D. diss., Vanderbilt University, 1981.

Hill, Patricia. "The New Black Aesthetic as a Counterpoetics: The Poetry of Ethridge Knight." Ph.D. diss., Stanford University, 1977.

Hoetink, H. *Slavery and Race Relations in the Americas*. New York: Harper and Row, 1973.

Hughes, Langston. "The Negro Artist and the Racial Mountain." *The Nation* (June 23, 1926): 692–94.

Innes, C. L. "Through the Looking Glass: African and Irish Nationalist Writing." In *African Literature Today*, no. 9 (1978): 10–24.

Irish, James. "Notes on a Historic Visit: Nicolás Guillén in Jamaica." *Caribbean Quarterly* 21, nos. 1 and 2 (1975): 74–84.

Jackson, Richard L. "The *Afrocriollo* Movement Revisited." *Afro-Hispanic Review* 3, no. 1 (1984): 5–10.

———. *The Afro-Spanish-American Author: An Annotated Bibliography of Criticism*. New York: Garland, 1980.

———. *The Black Image in Latin American Literature*. Albuquerque: University of New Mexico Press, 1976.

———. "Black Latin American Literature and Humanism." *Caribe*, April 1980, 18–21.

———. "The Black Novel in Latin America Today." *Chasqui* (1987).

———. *Black Writers in Latin America*. Albuquerque: University of New Mexico Press, 1979.

———. "*Chimurenga*: Literature and Black Liberation in Spanish America." In *Repression and Liberation in Latin America*, edited by J. Nef, 17–26. Ottawa: CALACS, 1981.

———. "The Human Legacy of Black Latin American Literature." *College Language Association Journal* 30, no. 2 (1986): 154–70.

———. "Literary Blackness and Literary Americanism: Toward an Afro Model for Latin American Literature." *Afro-Hispanic Review*, 1, no. 2 (1982): 5–11.

————. "Myth, History, and Narrative Structure in Manuel Zapata Olivella's *Changó, el gran putas.*" *Revista/Review Interamericana* 13, nos. 1–4 (1987).

————. "Coming Full Circle: The Polemical Trajectory of Modern Literary *americanismo.*" *Inter-American Review of Bibliography* 36, no. 3 (1986): 285–97.

Jahn, Janheinz. *Muntu: An Outline of the New African Culture.* Translated by Marjorie Grene. New York: Grove Press, 1961.

Johnson, Lemuel. "Issues in the Aesthetics of Populism and a Black Aesthetic." Paper presented at the National Council for Black Studies Conference, Ohio State University, Columbus, Ohio, February 16–19, 1977.

————. " 'El tema negro': The Nature of Primitivism in the Poetry of Luis Palés Matos." In *Blacks in Hispanic Literature: Critical Essays,* edited by Miriam DeCosta, 123–36. Port Washington, N.Y.: Kennikat Press, 1977.

Kubayanda, J. B. "Afrocentric Hermeneutics and the Rhetoric of *transculturación* in Black Latin American Literature." In *Latin America and the Caribbean: Geopolitics, Development, and Culture,* 226–40. Ottawa: CALACS, 1983.

————. "Hispanic Humanism and Nineteenth-Century Cuban Blacks: An Historico-Literary Perspective." *Plantation Society* 1 no. 3 (1981): 343–63.

King, Lloyd. "Nicolás Guillén and *Afrocubanismo.* In *A Celebration of Black and African Writings,* edited by Bruce King and Kolawole Ogung-Besan, 30–45. Zaria and Ibadan, Nigeria: Ah Madu Bello University Press, 1975.

Klotman, Phillis R., et al., eds. *Humanities Through the Black Experience.* Iowa: Kendal Hunt Publishing Co., 1977.

Lester, Julius. "Growing Down." *Change* 2 (1979): 34–37.

Lewis, Marvin. *Afro-Hispanic Poetry 1940–1980: From Slavery to Negritude in South American Verse;* Columbia: University of Missouri Press, 1983.

Liddell, Janice Lee. "The Whips Corolla: Myth and Politics in the Literature of the Black Dispora: Aimé Césare, Nicolás Guillén, Langston Hughes." Ph.D. diss., University of Michigan, 1978.

Lorenz, Gunter. "Adalberto Ortiz." Interview in *Diálogo con América Latina.* Valparaíso: Ediciones Universitarias de Valparaíso, 1972.

Luis, William, ed. *Voices from Under: Black Narrative in Latin America and the Caribbean.* Westport, Conn.: Greenwood Press, 1984.

Martin, Dellita. "Oral Traditions and *Biografía de un Cimarrón.*" Unpublished manuscript.

Miller, R. Baxter, ed. *Black American Literature and Humanism.* Lexington: University Press of Kentucky, 1981.

Mullen, Edward J. *Langston Hughes in the Hispanic World and Haiti.* Hamden, Conn: Anchor Books, 1977.

Navarro, Osvaldo. "Guillén, joven también." *El Caimán barbudo,* March 1977, 13.

Newman, Ronna. "Life and Works of Adalberto Ortiz." Ph.D. diss., Northwestern University, 1981.

Ojo-Ade, Feme. "De origen africano, soy cubano: African Elements in the Literature of Cuba." *African Literature Today,* no. 9 (1978): 47–57.

Olinto, Antonio. "The Negro Writer and the Negro Influence in Brazilian Literature." *African Forum* 2, no. 4 (1967): 5–19.

Pederson, Carl, Jr. "Main Trends in the Contemporary Colombian Novel, 1955–1967." Ph.D. diss., University of Southern California, 1971.

Perkins, Eugene. "The Changing Status of Black Writers." *Black World,* June 1970, 95.

"El poeta Nicolás Guillén, de paso por Madrid." *ABC,* July 24, 1970, 45.

Portuondo, José Antonio. Prologue to *Tengo,* translated by Richard J. Carr, 9–17. Detroit: Broadside Press, 1974.

Rassner, Ronald M. "Palmares and the Freed Slave in Afro-Brazilian Literature." In *Voices from Under: Black Narrative in Latin America and the Caribbean,* edited by William Luis, 201–21. Westport, Conn.: Greenwood Press, 1984.

Richards, Henry. "Entrevista con Nelson Estupiñán Bass." *Afro-Hispanic Review* 4, nos. 2 and 3 (1985): 34–35.

Sanchez, Reinaldo, et al. *Homenaje a Lydia Cabrera.* Miami: Ediciones Universal, 1978.

Senghor, Léopold Sédar. *Négritude et humanisme.* Paris: Editions du Seuil, 1964.

Shapiro, Norman R., ed. and trans. *Negritude: Black Poetry from Africa and the Caribbean.* New York: October House, 1970.

Silenieks, Juris. "The Maroon Figure in Caribbean Francophone Prose." In *Voices From Under: Black Narrative in Latin America and the Caribbean,* edited by William Luis, 115–26. Westport, Conn.: Greenwood Press, 1984.

Smart, Ian. *Central American Writers of West Indian Origin: A New Hispanic Literature.* Washington, D.C.: Three Continents Press, 1984.

———. "*Changó, el gran putas,* una nueva novela poemática." In *Ensayos de literatura colombiana,* edited by Raymond L. Williams, 149–56. Bogotá: Plaza y Janes, 1985.

———. "Nicolás Guillén's *son* Poem: An African Contribution to Contemporary Caribbean Poetics." *College Language Association Journal* 23, no. 3 (1980): 352–63.

————. "Religious Elements in the Narrative of Quince Duncan." *Afro-Hispanic Review* 1, no. 2 (1982): 27–31.

————. Review of *Changó, el gran putas*, by Manuel Zapata Olivella. *Afro-Hispanic Review* 3, no. 2 (1984): 31–32.

————. "Some Thoughts on the African Contribution to Spanish American Literature." *Ufahamu* 7 (1977): 73–91.

Snyder, Emile. "The Problem of Negritude in Modern French Poetry." *Comparative Literature Studies*. Special issue, edited by Haskell M. Block (1963): 101–14.

Tittler, Jonathan. "*Juyungo*/Reading Writing." In *Voices from Under: Black Narrative in Latin America and the Caribbean*, edited by William Luis, 165–80 Westport, Conn.: Greenwood Press, 1984.

Turner, Doris J. "Symbols in Two Afro-Brazilian Literary Works: *Jubiabá* and *Sortilégio*." In *Teaching Latin American Studies*, edited by Miriam Williford and J. Doyle Castell, 41–58. Gainesville, Fla.: Latin American Studies Association, 1977.

Williams, Lorna. "Carlos Guillermo Wilson and the Dialectics of Ethnicity in Panama." *Afro-Hispanic Review* 4, nos. 2 and 3 (1985): 11–16.

————. "Nicolás Guillén and the Poetic Response to the Cuban Revolution." Paper read at a Seminar in Atlantic History and Culture at Johns Hopkins University, February 27, 1979.

————. *Self and Society in the Poetry of Nicolás Guillén*. Baltimore: Johns Hopkins University Press, 1982.

Williams, Shirley Anne. *Give Birth to Brightness*. New York: Dial Press, 1972.

Wright, Richard. "Blueprint for Negro Literature." In *Amistad 2*, edited by John A. Williams and Charles F. Harris, 3–20. New York: Vintage Books, 1971.

Wynter, Sylvia. "Creole Criticism: A Critique." *New World Quarterly* 5 (1973): 12–36.

————. "Ethno or Socio Poetics." *Alcheringa*, edited by Michael Benamou and Jerome Rothenberg, 78–94. Boston: Boston University Press, 1976.

Zea, Leopoldo. "Negritude e indigenismo." *Cuadernos americanos* 197, no. 6 (1973): 16–30.

Index